Whole,
Single,
Free,
ME!

Whole, Single, Free, ME!

An Escape from Domestic Abuse

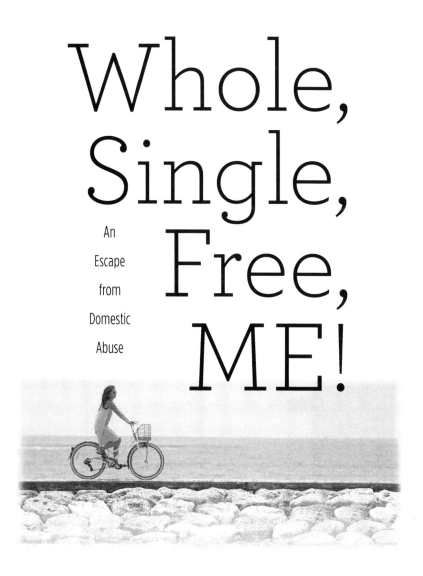

KATHRYN M. WOHNOUTKA, OFS

Dedicated to my family and friends,
who were my companions and support on my journey
of recovery to become a single, whole, free, ME!

And to my Heavenly Father who guided me
and made all of this possible.

CONTENTS

INTRODUCTION

Over the years I have come to know that my inner self is a teacher and that my divine mission is to lead others to healing and to a closer relationship with God as well as to share my sufferings and the tools I have used to grow in my own intimacy with God. Please accept this gift to you and pass on to others whatever you learn in these pages. Let us pray a beautiful prayer by Susanna Wesley:

> Help me, Lord, to remember that religion is not to be confined to the church . . . nor exercised only in prayer and meditation, but that everywhere I am in Thy presence. So, may my every word and action have a moral content. May all the happenings of my life prove useful and beneficial to me. May all things instruct me and afford me an opportunity

of exercising some virtues and daily learning and growing toward Thy likeness . . . Amen.[1]

(KLINE 42)

Blessings,
Kathy

Let us begin with a story about one right decision followed by a wrong decision that led me into twenty years of abuse. Eventually God was faithful to His promise in Romans 8:28 and turned all things to good because I do love him, and I am called according to His purpose.

The right decision was not to have an abortion, saving the life of my baby. The wrong decision was to marry my baby's father, who was already abusing me, rather than giving my baby up for adoption. At the time, I was naïve and searching for love. I was sure that all my boyfriend needed was someone who loved him enough, and then he would stop hitting me.

I wrote this story years later when I was wiser and had a clearer picture of God's plan in my life. The story shows how this one right decision, preserving the life of my child, had a positive effect on the lives of many others and helped to redeem all the years of abuse.

CHOOSING LIFE

With each year that passes, I become more convinced that abortion is wrong. My primary reason for feeling so strongly

---

1 Donald L. Kline *Susanna Wesley: God's Catalyst for Revival* (Lima, OH: C.S.S. Publishing, 1980) 42. Taken from Richard Foster, *Streams of Living Water* (San Francisco: Harper, 1989), 237.

*that abortion is wrong could be summed up in one word—Bill.
Bill is my son. I had the choice of an abortion. Each day as I
watched him grow closer to manhood, I thanked God that I
did not end his life.*

*During my first year in college, I became pregnant. My
mom's best friend married because she was pregnant and gave
up her dream of becoming a nurse. While my family lived in
Fort Morgan, we visited with my mom's friend's family often.
I saw mom's friend take out all her anger and unhappiness on
her oldest son. She blamed him for things that happened in
the family even if he had nothing to do with it. My mother was
convinced I should not marry my baby's father as her friend
had done. She gave me the option of having an abortion, which
was illegal at the time, or going to a home for unwed mothers
and giving my baby up for adoption. I immediately said I did
not want an abortion. I felt something inside me telling me that
abortion was wrong. My mom made plans for me to go into a
home for unwed mothers. However, my boyfriend's parents
intervened. My boyfriend and I were married a few days later,
and I was able to keep Bill.*

*As I have watched my son grow, adding both pleasure and
pain to my life, I have become more and more convinced that I
made the right decision. I believe that abortion was pushed on
me as an easy way out of a difficult situation. I had not been
given any information on birth control and was sent to college
with only my "good girl" morals to protect me.*

*Unfortunately, my morals were not enough, and I gave in to
temptation; nature did the rest. I felt then and feel even more*

strongly today that it is important to take responsibility for my actions. Abortion would have been a way of not accepting responsibility for my actions and getting out of a difficult situation without giving any consideration to Bill's right to life. Bill made my life more difficult at times, but I was responsible for his conception and owed him a chance at life.

I often think about the other people Bill has had an effect on through his life. At the age of fifteen, while a counselor-in-training at YMCA Camp Cullen, he saved a child from drowning after a terrible water-skiing accident. The child was hit in the head with a ski and was lying facedown in the lake. Bill tore off his life jacket, dove out of the boat, and swam to the child. The counselor drove the boat back to shore for help, leaving Bill and the child alone in the water. The child was not breathing and had turned blue by the time Bill reached him.

Luckily, Bill was a strong swimmer. While treading water, he turned the child over and gave him mouth-to-mouth resuscitation for several minutes until help came. What would have happened to that child if Bill had not been there? Would someone else have reacted with the same swiftness and skill as Bill?

The following summer while in Ecuador with a group called Amigos,[2] *Bill and his friends saved a local fisherman. The man had blown his hand off with a stick of dynamite while fishing. Bill and his friends drove the injured man over dirt roads to the*

---

2   Amigos de las Americas inspires summer volunteers age thirteen to twenty-two through collaborative community development and immersion in cross-cultural experiences in Latin America.

nearest hospital. Normally a four-hour drive, the boys covered the distance in two hours.

During the ride, Bill had to help with the tourniquet. While bouncing along at speeds in excess of 100 miles per hour, Bill, who was riding in the back of the pickup, showed remarkable courage. Every few minutes he had to climb on the roof of the cab and reach inside to hold the injured man's arm up while his partner released the pressure on the tourniquet. The driver did not slow down, and one of the other boys had to hold Bill's feet so that he would not fly off the cab. The boys managed to save the man's life and his arm. What would have happened if Bill had not been born? Would the man have bled to death or lost his arm?

Another exceptional rescue happened one day as Bill was driving home and saw a car go off the road into the bayou. He stopped, handed his wallet and watch to a person standing nearby, and asked them to put them in his truck. He then dove into the water. He was able to get the woman out of the car and safely to shore. He suspected she had a back injury and being a paramedic knew how to handle her so as not to cause permanent damage. When he returned to his truck, his wallet was not there. He had just cashed his paycheck so was quite worried. Later, he found out that the person had called his home and was holding on to the wallet so it would not be stolen.

As a frightened teenager, I could not foresee what effect Bill's birth would have on other people, but I am glad he has been there when others needed him. There have been many more cases over the years where Bill has intervened to save people's *lives. As an EMT, paramedic, and now an emergency room nurse, he saves lives often.*

There have been other situations in our family where the woman involved chose life even though others thought abortion was the best option. Bill's sister-in-law Kara and her husband saved their baby Kendall, who was born with spina bifida.[3] *The doctor told them she had an inch and a half gap in her spine and water on the brain and that they would be lucky if she lived three days. He said abortion was an option, but they wanted their baby. They came to George and me. We prayed with them and gave them a prayer blanket to put over the baby as Kara slept at night. Many prayers were said for the baby.*

By the time Kendall was born, the gap in her spine had almost closed. I gave them a baby-sized prayer blanket for her during the surgery to drain the water off her brain. We all waited outside the operating room until it was done. We have all had the joy of watching Kendall grow into a beautiful, intelligent young lady. She has competed in and won many beauty pageants, showing the world that people with disabilities are talented and valuable. She will soon graduate from high school, and I know she will go on to do extraordinary things.

My life has not always been easy. My choices have refined me and made me stronger and more forgiving. My choices have given me an inner strength that only comes from God.

---

3   Spina bifida is a birth defect in which an area of the spinal column does not form properly, leaving a section of the spinal cord and spinal nerves exposed through an opening in the back.

I am a child of God and run home to my Abba Father, Daddy God, to get the strength and guidance to do what He is calling me to do. Then I put on "the full armor of God" as it says in Ephesians 6:14–17:

> So stand fast with your loins girded in truth, clothed with righteousness as a breastplate, and your feet shod in readiness for the gospel of peace. In all circumstances, hold faith as a shield, to quench all [the] flaming arrows of the evil one. And take the helmet of salvation and the sword of the Spirit, which is the word of God.[4]

I know that through Him all things are possible—like this book that He is guiding me in writing. It is as a testimony to His glory, mercy, and saving grace in my life. Now let us go back to the beginning.

---

4   All Bible verses are from the New American Bible, Revised Edition (NABRE) translation, http://www.usccb.org/bible, 2011.

CHAPTER ONE

IN THE BEGINNING

> But where was I to start? The world is so vast. I shall start
> with the country I know best, my own. But my country is
> so very large. I had better start with my town. But my town,
> too, is large. I had best start with my street. No: my home.
> No: my family. Never mind, I shall start with myself!
>
> ~ *WIESE 135*

I was born May 14, 1950, on Mother's Day in Fort Morgan,
Colorado. I was my parents' first child and had been long
awaited. My dad named me (unbeknownst to my mom) for
two of his girlfriends, Leona Marie for beauty and Kathryn
Jewel for brains: Kathryn Marie. I have always loved my name.
We lived on my grandparents' farm. My grandfather had leu-
kemia and watched over me while my parents ran the farm.
He thought I was special because I had blue eyes like his, and
I was his first grandchild. He died when I was almost three.

This was the first significant loss in my life. It was a loss that took me many years into my adult life to deal with, but that story comes later.

My mother had James (Jim) Jr., the first of my four brothers, a few months before my grandfather's death, and the next brother, Robert, a quick fourteen months later. John came three years after that. My father had several severe crop losses, so he and my mother both had to leave the farm to find work. Steve came along seven years later.

As a child, I was a tomboy. Not because I wanted to be, but because I was always surrounded by boys. I was the oldest of five with four younger brothers, scores of male cousins, and many neighborhood boys. Since only boys were around to play with, I forgot my dolls and learned to play baseball and hide-and-seek and to ride a bike. I even asked for a boy's bike so I would fit in better. To the boys I was just another friend and pal. To this day, I still have many male friends, but I was always the sister, never the girlfriend.

My earliest memories of God were of the cool basement in the beautiful old stone Presbyterian Church where my Sunday school class met. I was so proud of the pretty construction paper shapes I received each Sunday for memorizing my lessons. I remember the white-and-gold cross for the Lord's Prayer, the blue tablet shape for the Ten Commandments, and the lamb for Jesus.

As I grew older, I took care of my three brothers when I was not in school. When I was nine, I knew we had no money. I did not expect anything on Christmas morning. I was so surprised when I got a beautiful set of miniature china dishes and a red sweater. I still have those dishes.

My dad took a job in Sheridan Lake, Colorado, in 1960 and we moved far away from the farm. It was very hard on my mom, as she had lived on the farm and in the same community all her life. Nevertheless, she followed my dad and taught me that wives sacrifice for their husbands and go where their husbands go.

Sheridan Lake held what would become one of my fondest memories: going to church camp. Although we were very poor, my mother always found the money for me to go. For eight years, I went each summer to the beautiful Colorado Rockies. At camp, I studied the Bible, was guided by spiritual people, and gradually built a strong faith in God.

As a teenager, I loved going to church. It was a retreat for me, a place where I felt accepted, happy, and loved. I always dreamed of marrying a missionary. The picture "Christ's Heart Door"[5] hung over the altar in our little church. The picture shows Jesus standing at the door and knocking from Revelations 3:20: "Behold, I stand at the door and knock. If anyone hears my voice and opens the door, [then] I will enter his house and dine with him, and he with me." It has always held a special place in my heart.

Much to my mother's dismay, our minster at the inter-denominational church we attended talked me into being baptized again. I had been baptized (sprinkled) as an infant in the Presbyterian Church in Fort Morgan. My maternal

5 Warner Sallman, artist.

grandpa was an elder and held the water at my baptism. It was a very special day for my parents, so my mom's feelings were hurt by my decision. But I was young and stubborn. I did not remember my infant baptism and wanted to experience this special event of immersion in the big pool in our little church. And it was an awesome experience; I felt as if I died as I went into the water and was reborn as I emerged.

In 1964, we moved to Alamosa, Colorado, where I graduated from high school. I still call Alamosa home. Not sure why, as I only spent five years there before I left for college, never to return to my parents' home for more than very brief visits. My high school years were hard. I was overweight and did not feel like I belonged most of the time. As I grew up, my mother constantly held out her best friend who had gotten pregnant right out of high school as an example of what could happen if I was not careful.

I was smart, so I joined the math club and was the only girl. I had a terrible crush on one of the boys. He was in the math club and on the Long John Tigers intramural basketball team. I used to go watch them play. When we were seniors, he came into the office where I was working as a staff aid and needed his locker combination. I memorized what the woman told him and after that put good luck cards and other things in his locker from time to time. I do not think he ever knew who did it. I was not in his circle of friends. Since I was never asked to any school dances, I asked one of the boys to the Sadie Hawkins[6] dance during my senior year and he said

---

6 Sadie Hawkins dance is a dance in which the girls ask the boys, and in the late sixties we wore "hillbilly dress" to the dance.

yes. We had a nice time. Two friends hanging out was what it amounted to, but I wanted romance, and that was not there. I had thought he would ask me to prom, but he did not. He asked another girl who seemed to always be one step ahead of me in everything. It hurt and I cried.

When one of the other boys heard what happened, he asked me to prom. My mom was sick, so my brother Jim and I went shopping. Because I was overweight and our town had very few shops, we only found two dresses that fit me. One was so beautiful but expensive. It cost $50, which was a lot of money in 1968. My folks gave in and I got the dress. I felt so beautiful.

The day of prom, my dad's service station called to say I had flowers there. At first, my mom and I thought they were from my date but were actually from a sophomore friend and came with a poem. He was struggling with feelings of depression and aloneness, which made my heart break. His reference to me in the last line of the poem made me grateful that I had been his friend. Here are a few lines from that poem:

> **The only thing that keeps me**
> **Out of the dark endless pit of insanity**
> **Is my day to day strength**
> **And the light of one smile.**

High school was tough for me. One of the hardest things was being "mooed" at as I walked down the hall between classes. Even now, the memories make me sad. It was a particular young man who mooed at me and then he would laugh with his friends. In today's world this would be called bullying, but back then I just pretended I did not hear it; I'd just keep walking down the hall and then cry secretly at home. Years later as I worked on healing Little Kathy, I forgave that young man. I wanted to tell him at our twentieth class reunion that I had forgiven him, but when I arrived, I learned that he had committed suicide. I continue to pray for him to this day.

At graduation, I would not let my mom take pictures. I really did not like having my picture taken since I was overweight. But I was so glad to be graduating. The day before, I stayed at school and helped in the office. Many of my fellow classmates went out and celebrated; they all got in big trouble as their celebration involved beer. As the good girl, I was in the office working. I was never part of the "in" crowd. Sometimes that was good, like the day before graduation, but it was also lonely.

CHAPTER TWO

THE DARK YEARS
OF ABUSE

I went away to college at the Colorado School of Mines in 1968. There were eleven girls and four hundred guys in the freshmen class. With those odds, even an overweight girl had a chance, and I wanted someone to love me. Anyone!

I was only two weeks into college when I met Tom. He was exciting and liked me. I was on cloud nine. He was also very experienced sexually, while I, on the other hand, was not even sure how it was done! I guess I learned quickly, though, because in two months I was pregnant. Shortly after that, Tom started beating me. He was always so sorry afterward and twisted the circumstances so I believed it was my fault. I was terrified of him. He completely controlled me.

I was sure I could change him. He had told me he had an abusive childhood and my love was going to make everything better. In addition, my dad had always teased me by saying I should marry a man who beat me because I was a stubborn child. Therefore, I thought I deserved Tom's abuse. Many years later, when God restored my sanity, and I dealt with my childhood issues, I was finally able to confront and forgive my dad. He had been teasing me, but I took it to heart. Sad how teasing becomes part of our inner self, even when the message is wrong. My parents tried to intervene, but Tom's parents thought we should get married. After all, it was the right thing to do in our generation. His parents said they would support us and help Tom finish school. I quit school as my parents were no longer going to help me.

I remember the three days before the civil ceremony. We were looking for an apartment. My mind kept screaming, "I do not want to get married!" But fear, people-pleasing, intense pride, and teenage rebellion prevented me from doing anything to stop it. Even on the day we got married, I remember as we went before the judge, my mind was still screaming, *Do not do this!* Nevertheless, fear and pride won out. This was not the wedding of my dreams. Our few friends here at college where out of town for winter break, so we only had two strangers as witnesses at our marriage. My dreams of marrying a missionary and serving God together vanished.

Tom and I had been attending the majestic St. John's Episcopal Cathedral in downtown Denver while dating. Tom went through the motions and I thought he had faith in God. Worshiping together with my husband was still a very important part of my dream. So, after we were married, I joined the Episcopal Church.

As abusers do, Tom isolated me from my family, even sending back the money my parents sent to help us. After my son was born, I told him we were going somewhere and then we disappeared for a few hours. I actually met my mom, grandma, and great-grandfather. We had a five-generation photo taken.

I was gone too long, and Tom was very angry when I got back. He yelled at me and demanded to know where I had been. I lied and said we were shopping and I had lost track of time. He did not believe me and hit me, but I did not tell him the truth. And I was not sorry. My great-grandfather died shortly after the photo was taken. The bruises went away but I still have the photo.

We lived in an apartment next door to a Colorado state patrolman and his wife and young daughter. We got to be friends and they even became my son's godparents. They often heard my screams and the man did try to talk to Tom, but Tom was just more careful and made me be quiet when he hit me.

Tom was always worse in times of stress. We occasionally drove to his parents' home in Arizona. We would drive all night, eating only on his schedule, and I would have to drive after he was too tired to drive anymore. I was also tired because I could not sleep while he drove. I had to keep Bill entertained and quiet. It was a miracle I never had an accident. He also would yell and hit Bill if he got fussy and tired of being in his car seat. One night as we were driving, he got mad about me dropping something. He pulled over to look for it but could not find it so started hitting me with a flashlight. A state patrol officer happened to be driving by and thought the flickering light was a gunshot. He turned around and asked a lot of questions. At least the beating stopped. Of course, I was too terrified to say anything that might get Tom in trouble.

I worked for a few months at a café during Tom's senior year in college. One day I came to work with a black eye. I do not remember the reason he had hit me. One customer asked me on a date. I said I was married, and I will never forget his surprise. He pointed to my black eye and said he thought I had left my husband. I said no, you do not understand. In hindsight, I think he did understand that the abuse was wrong better than I did. But domestic abuse was something most people did not talk about in the 1960s.

You might ask why I did not leave my husband as my customer thought I should have. Well, my mom had taught me that you stay with your husband even in the bad times, and Tom had convinced me that I could not do anything on my own. Moreover, my pride kept me from admitting to anyone, including my parents, that I had made a mistake in marrying Tom.

There were too many incidents of abuse for me to write in this book, but some do stand out more in my memories than others do. For example, one day we went to buy baby furniture. We got everything picked out and then went to pay for our purchases. The store would not take Tom's out-of-state check, and back then credit cards were not the norm. Tom was very angry, and when we got in the car, I said that it was okay and we could go to another store after his parents sent us money to cover the cost. He started yelling at me, "It is all your fault!

You took too long picking out the crib and bedding." Of course that had nothing to do with the store not accepting his check, but he still made it my fault. He started hitting me and I put my head down to protect my face. He grabbed my long hair and started pulling it all out. I had a bald spot in the back for a long time.

After Tom graduated from the Colorado School of Mines in 1972, we moved to California. I was not the only one he beat. Our son was often the recipient of his father's uncontrollable anger. My worst memory was one day when Bill was almost four and went to an Easter egg hunt at the park. Bill was a shy child back then. All the other children and parents were running and grabbing eggs, which scared him, so he just clung to me. Tom got mad that he would not participate, and he dragged him back to the car. Then he started hitting him and hitting him. I could not get him to stop. It was terrible and still makes me cry to this day. Tom just kept saying his dad would not have taken the time to take him to an Easter egg hunt. It was always about what he wanted. Child abuse was not generally reported in the 1970s.

For about three years, every time Tom got mad at me while we were in the car, he would grab the inside of my leg just above the knee and pinch. I had a huge bruise there all the time, and even years later my leg showed a shadow where the bruises had been. One day we were visiting his parents and going somewhere. His mother was in the back seat with me and saw the terrible bruise when I got in the car. I just told her I fell. I usually wore slacks so the bruises would not show, but that day I was wearing a dress. Tom finally stopped squeezing my leg when we moved to Saudi Arabia. We did not have a car there.

Lying was a very big part of my life. Lying to others to cover up the abuse, lying to Tom whenever I agreed that whatever was making him angry was my fault so he would stop hitting me, but mostly lying to myself that each abuse incident would be the last. He was always so sorry afterwards. The pattern is called the "dance of abuse": The tension builds in the abuser, the incident happens, and then comes the "honeymoon" period when the abuser is sorry. Tom would give me flowers and gifts, take me out, and convince me the abuse would not happen again. Life was good for a while, and then the cycle started again.

A close friend asked me to be one of her bridesmaids, which set off another abuse incident. Since I had not had a wedding nor had ever been in one, I was so excited. I had a beautiful light green dress with embroidered daisies on it. It was full and light and made me feel beautiful.

Tom was always isolating me. Isolation is one of the tools the abuser uses to keep control. He decided he wanted to go to his folks that weekend and demanded I withdraw from the wedding at the last moment. It was always about what he wanted. I refused. Later he went out and got drunk, and when he came home, he hit me and raped me. He told me I was a whore like the young woman who was getting married the next day. He went to his folks the next day with Bill, our then five-year-old son, and, yes, I was in the wedding. I wish

I had the picture that was taken as I left the church; my friend said I was glowing. Despite the pain and humiliation I had to endure, I did feel beautiful that day walking down the aisle.

I longed to go back to college. Tom always stopped me, but my dream would not die. I started taking a couple of classes at California State University. I was so enjoying learning, growing, and making friends. Of course, Tom was not happy about me growing and having friends. In 1975, he took a job in Saudi Arabia to stop me from going to school. Saudi Arabia was a place where women were second-class citizens and was far from my new friends. But just as I had been taught by my mother, I put my dreams on hold and followed him.

Living in Saudi was like living in Disneyland. It was not real. We lived on a compound and "Mama Aramco," the company Tom worked for, took care of everything. Aramco employees picked us up at the airport and took us to a furnished house with groceries and all we needed. A few weeks later after our belongings arrived, we moved into camp and the company did the moving for us. We had gardeners and a houseboy who did the yard- and housework for us. Since women could not work, I busied myself with Bill, my son, and social activities. I chaired a large bazaar to raise money to send to charities around the world. I also led shopping tours to the Al-Hofuf Souk (a market).[7]

Living in a camp with a tall fence all the way around gave us all a false sense of security. Unfortunately, every now and

---

7   Al-Hofuf, also known as Al-Hasa, is the major urban center in the Al-Hasa Oasis in the Eastern Province of Saudi Arabia. Al-Hasa is also one of the largest date producers in the world and is known for its old souks (markets) and palaces.

then, reality had a way of waking me up to the fact that I was not in my home country and maybe not as safe as I thought. Bad things happened but the company hushed them up. People were sometimes flown out immediately. The company provided stills to make illegal liquor like moonshine. If you made the mistake of selling to the Saudi citizens and they got mad at you, you could find yourself on a plane with only a moment's notice. Sometimes the company did not get advance warning, and the person ended up in a Saudi jail. Not a good place. No bathroom, just a hole in the floor. No food or bedding. And you might be flogged until the company could get you released and fly you out. Tom made beer and cider for his own use and bought stronger liquor from a friend who ran a still, so his drinking and the abuse continued even in a country where liquor was illegal. Another incident I knew of was a friend's young son, only seven, being grabbed and raped on his way to school. The company quietly turned the Pakistani worker over to the Saudi authorities who flogged the worker and deported him.

Aramco tried to keep us happy by bringing in all kinds of entertainment, including famous Las Vegas comedians, singers like Kenny Rogers, and musicians from Europe. On one of my birthdays, we had front-row seats to see Jerry Lee Lewis. They also brought in star sport figures to do sport camps for the high school students when they were home from school. The company sent the high school kids out to school to good private schools so they did not have to provide education for them.

Depression was real around the holidays for all us, since we were so far from home and family. There were no Christmas lights, songs, or decorations in the stores. The first year we were there, a group of residents put on a Nativity play. Workers built a set representing the city of Bethlehem with the choir singing from on top of the props like the angelic choir singing from the heavens. Mary rode a real donkey and shepherds appeared with a few real sheep. It was magnificent when the wise men came in on real camels in their beautiful robes. Unfortunately, too many Saudis and their families came to watch, so the government shut it down. The play was one of my favorite memories of living there.

While in Saudi Arabia, I gave birth to our second child, my long-desired girl, Susan Marie. I had had two miscarriages before her. It took two long stays in the hospital and many months in bed to carry her to term. Since she was my second child, and I had helped at home with my younger brothers, I became the mother or big sister to all the young women who were having their first child. The culture in Saudi Arabia required breastfeeding and cloth diapers. The hospital sent the new moms home without any instructions on bathing or taking care of the baby, and phoning home to the States in those days was not an option.

Just after I had Susan by cesarean section, I got an infection in the hospital. When I got out of the hospital, we had to move a few days later into a three-bedroom home. Tom was off bowling and doing other things while I tried to pack everything. I was supposed to be resting and healing, but he was never there to do the packing. This was our twelfth move in eight years of marriage. I remember sitting on the floor, crying in pain and fatigue, with Bill trying to help me pack. I so was exhausted. Bill was only seven.

The abuse continued in Saudi, and Bill remained a target of Tom's temper. Bill learned to lie as a mode of self-protection. One of the worse days for me was our last Christmas there. Tom had told me many times he did not want anything for Christmas. He said Bill and I did not need to take the bus for the four- to six-hour trip to the Arab souk to shop. Moreover, there was not much to buy anyway when you got there. Plus, I would have had to take Bill, because at seven, he was a "man," and women could only go with a man to the men's souk. So, I did not get him anything. When Christmas Day came, Tom threw a tantrum all day, yelling at all of us, throwing things, and being abusive. In addition, of course, he made it out to be all my fault. My heart really hurt for the kids. In hindsight, staying in my marriage for the sake of my children did terrible damage to them—this is guilt I will always carry.

After three years, Tom just quit his job one day and we returned home to the United States. Following one very tough year of adjustments and living in four different places, we moved into our home in Houston in January 1979. Abuse, fear, and isolation filled the next twelve years. Gradually, the abuse in my marriage caused me to shut down all my feelings, including my feelings for God. My faith dried up and seemed to disappear. My pride caused me to withdraw further and further into denial. The locust of abuse ate away at my life. I lost myself and who I was. I just pretended I had the perfect family. Never admitting to anyone, even myself, that I had made a mistake, I tried to be the perfect mom, attending all of Bill and Susan's school and other activities. I was always pitching in to help and trying to find some sort of purpose to my life. For most of those years, I was a robot.

Then I started looking for ways out of my unhappy coma. In 1980, I became involved in the local civic association and undertook a project to compare possible cable television companies for our subdivision. The cable company the association chose was impressed with my final report and the understanding of franchising cable television I had attained during the process. They offered me a job working with other subdivisions and I took it. I had my own office and company car. I got to dress up and do something challenging outside the home. I was successful and procured many large franchise contracts. However, Tom did not like me working outside the home. I was changing, coming alive and realizing I could do something to take care of myself and earn a living. Tom forced me to resign just five months after I took the job, using Susan as the reason. She was only three.

CHAPTER THREE

THE BEGINNING
OF THE END

In 1982, Tom and I were part of starting a small mission church. The rector encouraged the women of the church to start a Daughters of the King[8] chapter. I went to the meeting to see what DOK was. The person in charge gave us a small pamphlet. She explained that all we needed to do was come to three meetings and we could be a Daughter and receive our silver cross. I had no clue why I was there and definitely did not feel called to become a Daughter; I just went along with the crowd and our priest's wishes. I attended my three meetings and got my cross in August 1982. We promised to pray daily and wear our crosses at all times. I did not know that the faithful prayers of this group would someday be answered by God's lifesaving grace and restoration of my life.

---

8   The Order of the Daughters of the King® (DOK) is a women's prayer order started in 1885 in the Episcopal Church. A Daughter pledges herself to a lifelong program of prayer, service, and evangelism. The Order spread to the Roman Catholic Church in 1986 and now also includes Anglicans and Lutherans.

As God started to relight that tiny spark of faith I still had down deep in my heart, I started to grow in the DOK. My abusive husband became more and more resentful. He demanded I quit Daughters and not wear my cross. I finally drifted away from DOK and the church for a while.

Tom always totally controlled our finances as another way of isolating me. I had to tell him every penny I spent. Then he would add it all up and tie it to his salary. It had better match! One time Susan needed a dress for her piano recital. I found a sweet blue-and-white dress on sale for $12. When I bought it, it triggered an abuse incident. After it was over, Tom went out and a bought both Susan and me necklaces. The cost of the two necklaces was $1,200. We could not afford them, but it was okay because he bought them. Susan and I later gave them away as part of our healing.

When the oil bust happened in 1982, Tom was laid off. He came home and yelled at me to get a job. With no college degree or training, I could only get a low-paying job working customer service at a cable television company. I was so lonely and empty inside. I put on such a great front that the people at work called me Betty Crocker. They thought I had the perfect life: a beautiful home, two wonderful children, a good job, and a handsome, successful husband. I was also a good cook, always bringing goodies to work, especially my banana bread and peanut butter balls.

My coworkers started inviting me to happy hours, and I went, hoping to find happiness or at least forget the misery at home. This was another step in my awakening and led to a serious flirtation with a coworker. He told me that I did not deserve abuse, that I deserved better. He started awakening feelings in me I had not felt for a long time. I felt alive for the first time since I had married. I did not know how to handle the feelings. I felt like I was exploding inside. The loneliness was getting worse, and now there was anger mixed with the fear. However, I found the happy hours to be as empty as my life.

Then, I received a call one day inviting me to a Daughters of the King luncheon on a Saturday and decided to go. When I entered the church, I had an overwhelming feeling of coming home. I asked for God's forgiveness. I quit going to the happy hours and asked God to help me in my marriage. My sisters in the Daughters of the King began praying for my marriage too.

I started secretly seeing a counselor who worked with battered women. She insisted I attend Al-Anon meetings, a twelve-step program that helps members come to understand that problem drinking is a family illness that affects everyone in the family. She stressed that I had to attend not just once but at least six meetings before I decided if Al-Anon was for me. I put off going to the meetings. What would I tell Tom?

At home, the battering continued. Tom had quit church altogether. He could not stand for me to have friends or outside activities. He would not allow me to wear my Daughters of the King cross. He called my prayer sisters names and The Order a cult. He tore up my Bible and threatened me on many occasions. I wore my DOK cross at work but took it off before coming home.

One day I forgot to take it off. When I walked in the back door, Tom was standing a few feet away. He screamed that if he ever saw that cross again, he would destroy it. A black aura seemed to engulf the room. I felt like I was facing Satan himself, but Tom did not touch my cross or me that day. Only later did I realize that Tom never hit me when I was wearing my cross. Strange . . .

Things continued to deteriorate. One of Tom's coworkers who went to church with me called and told me that Tom was spending a lot of time with someone from his office. She confirmed my own suspicions that he had a girlfriend. Tom was still abusing alcohol, and the doctor was "helping" his depression with prescription antidepressants. As I was praying for a way out of this dilemma, a friend suggested I take my children and run away. I had tried to leave before but he always threatened to kidnap the children, or worse. It sounded crazy at first, but as I discussed the idea with my therapist, priest, and other sane people, it became clear it was the only answer. I now realize it was God's answer.

In late August 1986, I secretly started making plans to run away. I planned a trip to New York City to look for a job. Tom thought the trip was a business trip. My company gave me a good reference and had set up a job interview with their sister company in New York City. A few days before, Tom had attempted suicide. I honestly thought he was going to kill me when he came to the bedroom and woke me up after pulling the phone out of the wall and locking the door. He had been talking to his girlfriend on the phone for several hours. She had rejected him. He announced that he was going to commit suicide and wanted me to sit with him.

He took an overdose of his antidepressants, washing them down with wine. As he laid there, I was terrified of what he might do next, but managed somehow to sit calmly on the edge of the bed. I was too afraid to try and stop him. My mind was trying to figure out what to say to make him stop without making him mad. He told me that if only I had loved him more, everything would be okay. I just sat there and listened. He took another bunch of pills and finally passed out.

I unlocked the door, went out, and told our son Bill, who was now seventeen, that his dad had taken an overdose. Bill had returned home from work while I was locked in the bedroom. He said, "Let him die, Mom, it will solve all our problems." I thought about it, but even in my sick state, I knew that was murder, so I called the paramedics. Tom had taken enough pills to do the job and almost succeeded. The doctors worked for several hours before he was stable. The next day the doctors and I argued with him, and, finally, about 6:00 p.m. Saturday evening he committed himself to the psychiatric hospital. At church the next day my Daughters of the King group rallied around me. I was completely exhausted. I turned my whole life over to God and prayed all through the service for His guidance. I truly surrendered my life to Him. Questions kept going through my mind as my favorite song, "I am the Bread of Life"[9] by Suzanne Toolan, was being sung during the Eucharist.

---

9 "I am the Bread of Life" is a Christian hymn composed by Sr. Suzanne Toolan in 1966. It is based on the Bread of Life discourse in the Gospel of John chapters 6 and 11.

Could I go on my trip and leave Tom in the hospital? Was New York where I should go? As I stood up to leave church, I heard a powerful voice say to me, "Everything will be okay with Scott."[10] I felt like a ton of bricks had been dropped on me. I had to sit back down. The voice was so strong; I knew it was God speaking to me. It was the reassurance I needed that the trip to New York was a correct decision. Scott worked for one of our providers and had been training me for the changes coming our way due to the upcoming scrambling of his company's cable television signal. We became friends through the training. He lived in New York City and was giving me advice on what hotel to stay at in New York and how to get to my interview. It was my first trip to New York and I was nervous about getting around. I went on the trip and the interview went well. I rode the subway for the first time and got to see two Broadway shows. I could not get a cab after the theater so I walked back to my hotel alone singing loudly "Onward Christian Soldiers." It was as if I was invisible. No one even seemed to notice me and I made it safely.

On Saturday, September 13, 1986, Scott showed me the Statue of Liberty and the World Trade Center. We went to the observation deck on the 107th floor of the South Tower and looked down on the Statue of Liberty. It was a beautiful, clear day. The sight was breathtaking. (Little did I know that in April 2001, almost fifteen years later, I would again look down on the Statute of Liberty from the ninety-eighth floor of the South Tower. I was there to teach a class. I never dreamed that in a few

---

10   Name changed

short weeks all my clients and coworkers who attended my class would die as both towers became rubble on September 11, 2001.)

I wanted to see the historic Trinity Episcopal Church. Scott did not know where it was, but as we were leaving the World Trade Center headed for other stops, there it was! Scott commented that he could see that God was guiding my life, just like I kept telling him.

After I returned home, Tom was released from the hospital and put on a different antidepressant, which made him even more violent. Every evening we argued over my not loving him enough. He kept saying, "If you only loved me more, everything would be okay." To be honest, I was so tired of all the drama; I could not even go through the motions anymore. I secretly continued to take steps to move to New York.

I was unable to function at work. One day I just could not stand it any longer and had to talk to someone. I pulled out the Al-Anon schedule my therapist had given me and saw that there was a beginner's meeting at 10:00 a.m. It was 9:30. I got up, told the department secretary that I was leaving, and went to the meeting. It was two meetings, each one hour long. The first hour was for beginners and the second hour was a regular meeting. I remember crying through the first hour and pouring out my story of abuse. All I remember of the second hour was this very serene woman sharing how she had grown in the program. Others were re-enforcing her feelings, and a flow of genuine love was there. This was a giant step forward in my recovery.

CHAPTER FOUR

RUNNING AWAY

By the end of September 1986, life was going from bad to worse. Tom was looking at guns on his way home from work and threatening to kill himself in front of our children. Every time things seemed to be a little better, and I would decide not to leave, he got worse. In late September 1986, the children and I could not take any more. The fear was too great. Even though the timing was three weeks ahead of when I planned to leave, I quit my job and called a mover. The counselor at the high school arranged for my son, who was a senior and did not want to go with me, to live with one of his teachers until he graduated. Bill had discussed his situation with his teacher, and she and her husband were willing to help him stay in Houston.

The night before the movers came, I sat on the edge of my bed, crying. My seventeen-year-old son, with his man-size body, towered over me. I said to him, "You do not know what it has been like to live in fear—no, not fear, *terror* for eighteen years! Your dad started beating me before we were married. I had married him out of fear and felt imprisoned, trapped, with no way out." Now I finally had the strength to leave.

I tried calling a few battered women's shelters in New York City to find my daughter and me a place to stay, but had no luck. On Wednesday, a member of my Daughters of the King prayer group called and said she knew of a family in Connecticut that would take us in. An answer to my prayers!

My feelings of guilt and responsibility for my husband were intense. Two days before leaving for New York, I was struggling with these feelings. I went to see my priest. While we were talking, God's voice spoke over my priest's voice and said to me, "You have done everything I told you to do." This gave me the peace and courage to go on. A serenity enveloped me, and I knew I was doing the right thing.

Thursday morning a friend from work, a neighbor, two of my son's friends, my children, and two movers frantically helped me pack up half my house and throw it into a moving van. I had never been able to do things simply! I always took along a lot of baggage.

We were halfway into the packing when my secretary, who was covering for me, called to tell me my husband had called. He left a message that he had just been laid off. I knew he had an appointment with his psychiatrist at 11:30. I told everyone to hurry things along and then called his doctor to explain that I was leaving and asked if she could please stall him so we would not have a scene at the house. She felt what I was doing was wrong, but she did not change my mind. We frantically finished throwing things into the van.

I packed my daughter, her hamster, our small dog, and any remaining belongings that would fit into my small Chevy Chevette. Now we were on our way to Connecticut. Many fears filled my mind. Was I doing the right thing leaving my son behind with his teacher? Where were we going? Would I be able to support us? Would any of my possessions, which we had just thrown frantically into a moving van, make it to our destination in one piece? Would Tom come home and commit suicide when he found us gone? I was so scared, but too scared to stay. Running away was the only way to save our lives. Only God could have arranged Tom's layoff and my leaving both on the same day. But then God had arranged everything so far, and I had to continue to trust Him.

I found out later that the doctor told my husband I had left. The double whammy of my leaving and his layoff helped him hit bottom. He was taken to a psychiatric hospital from her office. Only God could have arranged the timing of all these events. My husband found Alcoholics Anonymous (AA) and recovery in the hospital.

My daughter and I drove as far as we could each day and then found a motel. The hamster could not stay in the car without air conditioning, so we went through many drive-in restaurants for our meals. The dog kept throwing up. It took four and half days to reach our safe house in Connecticut. I had only gotten maps for as far as New York, so I had to rely on God for the last few miles into Connecticut. There were no cell phones or Google Maps in 1986!

The couple we were staying with had their own story of God's grace to tell. At their church just a couple of weeks before, their priest had challenged the congregation to help others, especially battered women and their children. Three days later, they got the call from our mutual friend, who asked them if they would help us. You see, this couple had attended our little church of Christ the King in Houston before moving to Connecticut. God had prepared a place for us even before I knew I was leaving. The second day in Connecticut, I left my daughter with the wonderful couple who had taken us in and went to New York City to look for a place to live. God had been my constant guide and literally carried me this far, so I continued to trust Him. Surrendering my life to God had not meant that I would just sit and watch as my life went by. No, my job was to do the legwork. I had to provide the energy, determination, and hard work. As I drove down the interstate toward New York City, I had no idea where I was going. I just kept driving. When the sign for the New Rochelle exit appeared, I took it. At the time, I wondered if it was God's nudging or the familiarity of the name from *The Dick Van Dyke Show!* I drove up and down the main street praying for guidance. I was wondering where to go, and I asked God to send someone to help me.

I stopped at a realtor's office to see if they might have a small house for rent. They said they would look around and I should call them later. As I was leaving, I looked down at my tires for the first time since I had left Houston. The front tire was bald in several places. I got in the car and asked God where I should go for new ones. Not far down the street, I found a tire dealer. I stopped and while waiting for the new tires, a man approached me. I thought he was trying to pick me up. In hindsight, I know God had sent him to help me. After my tires were changed, we drove separately and met at a café. He had lived there all his life. After buying me a map, a local paper, and coffee, he told me which neighborhoods to look at, which ones to avoid, and where to find a hotel for the night. He gave me his card and suggested dinner. I said I would call him but never did. He had given me the direction I needed.

I began that evening to look at several different places to live. I had visualized a duplex with an elderly woman downstairs who could help watch after my daughter. The more I looked, the more I was aware that New York was not the place for my daughter and me. God placed a strong feeling of uneasiness on my heart. I would have to commute over two hours each way to work and Susan was only nine, too young for me to be so far from her. I returned to Connecticut late the next day and asked my daughter how she felt. She already loved Connecticut and wanted to stay there. The next day after more prayer I called my one pending job offer in New York City and told the man thanks but no thanks. God wanted us to stay in Connecticut. I know the man thought I was crazy.

Depression set in, making each day a struggle just to get up. But faith in God had carried me this far, and I made myself set a goal of three calls for jobs or houses per day. Finally, after two weeks I found the duplex with an elderly woman living downstairs. Although the rent was very high, and I still did not have a job, I took it on faith. Surprisingly the owner rented it to me without any questions. My furniture was delivered the next week and we settled in.

I had sold my company stock to pay for my escape, but my money was quickly running out. In fact, by Friday of that week I had less than fifty dollars and no job in sight. Then I received a call from the phone company asking me if I would like to go to work for them temporarily during a strike. I know God was working because I had not applied for the job. I had only told the man who took my application for phone service that I had customer service experience and needed a job. I guess he passed my name on to someone.

A soup kitchen existed at a nearby church that had an Al-Anon meeting after lunch. I went, had lunch, and stayed for the meeting. It was my second Al-Anon meeting and my first one in Connecticut. Because it was an afternoon meeting, all the other people were married women. I did not want to hear how happy they were. I had just left my husband and I wanted a divorce. However, I do remember their love and acceptance. I also took a meeting schedule. When I arrived home, there were two letters in the mail. Each had fifty dollars inside. One letter was from my mom and the other from a good friend. I had not asked for money; they just felt compelled to send it.

Monday, I started at the phone company, working side by side with all the managers. Due to the strike, they fed us breakfast, lunch, and dinner as well as snacks. This helped me out on groceries at home. My counselor in Houston had told me to attend six Al-Anon meetings before I decided if Al-Anon was for me. I decided Tuesday night to try a beginner's meeting listed in the schedule. The meeting helped me to know that I belonged in Al-Anon by teaching the importance of detachment and living a more sane life. I began attending as many meetings as possible.

When the strike ended, God provided a better job just five miles from my home at ESPN and a part-time job waiting tables. I was now able to make ends meet and keep a roof over our heads. In fact, my manager at ESPN had been looking for someone with my very specialized experience. I had trained with another company to prepare for the scrambling of their signal, a new procedure all the cable channel providers were using to stop theft and increase their revenues. While training with that company, I had met Scott and the trip was the ruse I used to go to New York City on "business." ESPN was setting up a center to convert all their customers to scrambling. My manager made the comment that "I had fallen out of the sky." Yes, I had! God again had prepared everything I needed in advance. God's love and grace continued to amaze me.

I wrote the following article for the Al-Anon magazine about a discovery I made while living in Connecticut. At the time I wrote the story I was still in denial about my marriage and not seeing things clearly. For years I had tried to convince others I had a perfect marriage and family. I needed time to heal and accept the reality of abuse. So when I say I had a loving husband, that was part of my denial and pretending.

HOW I DISCOVERED THE SOURCE OF MY LONELINESS

Why am I feeling so lonely? My husband and children are here in the house with me. All my friends are nearby or just a phone call away. I have everything a woman could want—a loving husband, two good children, many friends, and a beautiful home—so why do I have this deep loneliness? Is there a problem in my marriage? Doesn't my husband love me enough? Do all people feel this way or is there something the matter with me? These were thoughts and feelings I had frequently over the eighteen years I was married—feelings that hurt down to my depths and scared me. I was very afraid of being totally alone—of being on my own without my husband, so I stayed in my abusive marriage, shrouded in the veil of denial, rather than face my feelings of loneliness.

Finally, when my home situation became unbearable, I ran away for five months to Connecticut. I knew no one there and was afraid of being alone, but the fear for my life was stronger, so I went. A few weeks later, on a snowy afternoon as I sat on the edge of my bed in my new home, looking out the window at the squirrels scampering along the snow-covered tree branches, the feeling of loneliness, which had often haunted me in Houston, crept over me. I was surprised as I realized that I did not feel any lonelier here, by myself, than I had felt at home in Houston surrounded by family and friends. Why? This awareness started me on a search. Where was my loneliness coming from if it was worse when I was with people than when I was totally alone? Was something lacking in my relationships or was the problem inside of me?

I began to notice when and where I was when I felt lonely. Sometimes I felt the loneliest when I was with other people. I noticed that at these times I felt out of place or inferior.

Through the experience of writing my life story, I discovered that even as a young child I had very low self-esteem. As I explored the reasons for my feelings of low self-esteem, I discovered the source of my deep loneliness. I was the only girl in the family. I had always had my own room. In most of the houses we had, my room had been apart from the rest of the family. I remember one house where the sun porch, located off the living room and completely separate from the rest of the house, had been made into my room. Alone at night so far from everyone, I was afraid and felt isolated.

At the age of nine, I began taking care of my three younger brothers while my mother and father worked. My brothers looked on me as a surrogate parent. The overwhelming responsibility of their well-being made me feel separate from them. I stopped being a child.

In addition, during my childhood, we lived on a farm, so I had few playmates. We were very poor, and I often did not have needed school supplies or clothes. My shame over our poverty kept me from making friends at school and added to my feelings of isolation and low self-esteem. As I began to connect the discovery of my low self-esteem to my feelings of loneliness, I realized I had always felt very afraid, isolated, and alone as a child. My parents had each other, my brothers shared experiences, and there I was, all alone in my room, restricted in my relationships, and with low self-esteem which kept me from reaching out to my family and classmates. As the realization that my loneliness came from the deep feelings of isolation I had as a child, a great weight was lifted off me. The deep-down loneliness I had known for years disappeared with my new awareness, but my battle with loneliness was not over.

The awareness that I was not as lonely when alone as I was with people gave me a new confidence. I felt empowered to move forward with my single life and not be so afraid of being alone.

Now back to my story . . . While I was in Connecticut, Tom and I began to work on our problems long distance. He was going to Alcoholic Anonymous and I was going to Al-Anon. Although I was still scared of him, God gave me several signs that I should give my marriage another chance. I came to Houston to visit for Christmas and to see if we could work things out. It was the best Christmas we ever had. The Al-Anon motto "Keep It Simple" was my guide. The only decorations were the Nativity Scene, dinner consisted of just the four of us, and activities were limited to the midnight service at our church.

My daughter and I returned to Connecticut after Christmas. On January 23, 1987, my husband and son came to Connecticut so we could celebrate our eighteenth wedding anniversary and renew our wedding vows in a church ceremony. We had eloped, and I had always wanted to be married in the church. I had a lot of anxiety before my husband arrived. I knew if I went through with the ceremony, I would feel committed to the marriage and to returning home. I attended meetings and prayed constantly. My Al-Anon sponsor and friends were supportive. They thought I should give my marriage another chance because Tom had found recovery in AA and I had grown in Al-Anon.

It turned out to be God's will for me to go through with the ceremony although the weekend did not go smoothly. When I went to meet my husband and son at the airport, their flight from New York had been canceled. I assumed they would be on the next flight, so I waited several hours at the airport. Of course, these were in the days before cell phones. When they were not on that one, I drove the hour home only to arrive at 1:00 a.m. to the phone ringing. They had taken a bus from New York and were stranded several miles away in 15-below-zero weather. My car was on empty, and I did not know the area well, but off I went. Again, God was my guide, and by 2:30, we were home.

The ceremony was to take place after a church meeting and before my husband's plane left on Sunday. Time was critical. The church meeting dragged on and on. My husband had decided that if it did not end by 12:30, we would have to forget it. I still was not sure of God's will for me and our marriage, so I just sat there trusting Him and praying. The discussion in the meeting was going on and on, when suddenly at 12:25, the minister stood up, tabled all further discussion, and adjourned the meeting. As I renewed my wedding vows in the beautiful chapel, I knew it was time to go home to Houston. My time in Connecticut had been a good time for healing, but it was also difficult working two jobs, leaving Susan alone too much, and trying to pay the bills. Also I missed my son and truly felt Tom had changed, so I decided to go home. Maybe that is the bottom line: Houston was still home. And both of the kids wanted us to be a family again. Part of being an abused woman is a hope that life will change. The abuse will stop. And I did believe in staying in my marriage.

CHAPTER FIVE

RECONCILIATION

By the end of February 1987, Tom and I had reconciled. Susan and I returned to Houston to resume the life I had left, but my time in Connecticut had changed me. I was more independent and confident. Recovery had changed Tom too. The abuse stopped.

My returning home was also important for my son. Bill had struggled personally and in school while we were gone. Living with his teacher had not worked out. His teacher and her husband did not have children. They tried to build a family with Bill. It was too much for him. Bill escaped their home one night through a window and went back to live with his dad. I truly believe if I had not returned home when I did, he would not have graduated from high school.

Bill and Susan had always been close, so he was glad to have the sometimes "annoying" little sister home. Susan quickly settled back into her old school, Girl Scouts, and circle of friends. Houston was the only home she knew. We had moved there just before her second birthday. Connecticut had been an adventure for her but was also filled with moments of uncertainty and aloneness. She felt good about coming home. Tom and I were both working our AA and Al-Anon programs. I got a sponsor and developed many good friends in Texas Al-Anon. I continued to attend as many meetings as possible and read Al-Anon literature. Al-Anon changed me. I kept looking inside and working on healing and growing with the Holy Spirit's help.

During the summer, I attended a workshop by my favorite Guideposts[11] writer, Marion Bond West. I had followed her life through the pages of the Guideposts books and magazines for years. I used the Guideposts devotion books for my daily devotion and recorded something to be grateful for each day in the note section at the end of the month's readings. While in Connecticut Susan and I did it together. It was a special memory for both of us.

I was thrilled to get to meet Marion in person and hear more of her story. As she talked, a strange thing happened. A voice louder than hers said, "You will be a widow in two years." I knew it was God, but even so, a part of me doubted that I had really heard it. After all, I have always been good in mathematics, and tend to think in terms of numbers and facts, not dreams and visions. Nevertheless, I did tuck it away in my heart with a wait-and-see attitude.

---

11 Guideposts is a nonprofit organization dedicated to inspiring the world to believe that anything is possible with hope, faith, and prayer through books and magazines.

That summer, when I visited the University of Houston campus with my son on parents' weekend, I decided to go back to college to get my degree. I had given up this goal many years earlier when Tom moved me to Saudi Arabia. My husband had convinced me that I was too dumb and therefore had no reason to go to college. My low self-esteem had confirmed his assessment for many years. Now, with my new confidence, I felt I had to accomplish this long-time goal. I figured out that if I took two classes each semester, fall, spring, and summer, I would graduate with my bachelor's degree in eight years. EIGHT YEARS! It seemed like an eternity, an impossible goal with a full-time job, two active children, and an unsupportive husband. I had many doubts about being able to handle the studying and competing with younger students. After all, it had been twenty years since I had gone to school. I did not remember anything!

But I faced my doubts and fears and started the journey toward my goal. I applied at Houston Community College. Then I chose my classes and registered. I continued to do the legwork, never knowing if I could get there but only that I had to keep moving forward and leave the rest to God. It was not an easy path. Trying to balance work, family, and school left little time or energy; but through persistence and keeping my goal in sight, I gradually worked my way up the hill.

Through the summer of 1987, I continued to explore my feelings of loneliness and low self-esteem. Then one evening in September, I discovered the source of my low self-esteem. I was attending an Al-Anon group session where the topic for the evening dealt with getting in touch with your feelings. There were over one hundred people crowded in the room. Several people had volunteered to share painful memories from their childhood. As these brave volunteers were sharing terrible experiences of child abuse and neglect as well as their feelings associated with these experiences, I was thinking back to my own childhood and some of the recent memories I had been exploring over the last few months.

Our leader had asked us to just feel as the volunteers told their stories and not to judge. I thought about how I felt as the only girl in the family. I began to connect the discovery of my low self-esteem to my feelings of loneliness. As the participants were exploring the feelings that the volunteers' stories had aroused, I continued thinking about how I had felt deep down as a child. I realized I had always felt very afraid, isolated, and alone. In addition, the years of abuse had added to these feelings. Awareness can be very freeing, and, to my surprise, my low self-esteem and feelings of loneliness started disappearing. I continued to go deeper.

Through more therapy and a silent retreat in late 1987, I was able to recreate my very early childhood feelings. It was the first of what was to be many retreats at the Cenacle Retreat House[12] in Houston. My Daughters of the King group was

---

12   The Houston Cenacle was a welcoming, peace-filled place, a sanctuary for prayer, discernment, and spiritual growth. The original Cenacle Retreat House (building and grounds) in Houston where I spent many wonderful days at retreats and in spiritual direction was destroyed by Hurricane Harvey in August 2017. For a while, the Cenacle Sisters continued their ministry in a new location, but eventually passed their ministry on to a group of spiritual directors. See their website: https://emmausspiritualitycenter.com/.

having a quiet day and I went. My therapist had said that you could get back to feelings from your childhood even if you could not get back to the memories. I found a secluded place amongst the trees. I sat on a log and started asking Jesus to walk back through my life with me. We went back through my memories slowly. Then there were no more memories; I just sat in quiet prayer going deeper within myself. Suddenly, there was an explosion of pain—terrible feelings of fear, grief, confusion, dread over the future, and a huge feeling of abandonment overcame me. I started to sob. I had reached the time when my maternal grandfather—the only grandfather I ever knew—had died. I was almost three years old at the time, and though I had no memory of him, I still had the feeling of loss.

My mom had told me that he had leukemia and had turned over the family farm to my parents for them to run. He took care of me during the first two years of my life while my parents tended the farm. I was very special to him, his first grandchild, and I had his blue eyes. I realized that this loss had colored the rest of my life and drove my people-pleasing behavior and low self-esteem. I also realized I had never grieved my grandfather's death and blamed myself for his disappearance from my life. If I had been a good girl, he would not have left me.

The feelings that poured out that day told me that when he died, I did not understand where he had gone. I no longer felt safe. I felt abandoned. I developed a fear of the future. Would others leave me? In those sobs, all my life became clear. I had become a good girl, a people pleaser, because I could not trust that others would not leave me too. Little Kathy wondered if he left because she had done something wrong or was not good enough. Was it my fault? I had built a wall, a safe place, around myself to protect me from the pain of being abandoned. And I lived my life in fear and isolation from that point on. I would do anything to please people, even accepting abuse, because I was afraid of being abandoned again.

And I discovered that the years of abuse in my marriage had caused me to build the wall around Little Kathy higher and thicker until she was lost. At least she felt safe inside her wall where nothing could hurt her. I became a robot, going through life without feelings. I spent my time and energy trying to maintain the image of a perfect family. I tried to do all the right things. I buried all my feelings. When the problems in my marriage got so bad that I could no longer ignore them, my wall began to crack. In my pain, I turned to God and He sent people into my life to help me. Gradually, through the Al-Anon program and many caring people, I started to remove the bricks of my wall. Trust came slowly. Little Kathy was afraid of the changes, of being abandoned again. I still tended to say everything was okay and go on with a smile even when I was hurting inside.

In the summer of 1988, after the retreat where I began to tear down my wall, I had an overwhelming desire to visit my grandparents' graves. On a trip to Colorado, I made the seventy-mile side trip to where my grandparents were buried and put flowers on their graves. Suddenly, I started crying. I did not understand why I was crying. Later, I realized the tears came because I had opened enough of my wall to let "Little Kathy" feel her unmourned grief for my grandfather. With God's amazing love, I was able to heal a very deep hurt that had controlled much of my life.

In 1988, Tom's dad was diagnosed with pancreatic cancer and died in four months. His death was a terrible shock to all of us. WT (Bill), Tom's dad, had always been a wonderful, kind man to Bill, Susan, and me. Tom had told me he had been abusive, but I did not find that to be true during the time I knew him. I came to realize that Tom was spoiled by his grandmother who lived with them, so he thought his father's attempts at discipline was abuse. His mother, on the other hand, never liked me. Tom is more like her. I always found her cold, snobby, and cruel. She never believed Tom was an alcoholic or had abused me. He could do no wrong in her eyes.

Tom's mom was also cruel to Bill and Susan at times. Bill often mentions the time she deliberately walked on his new letter jacket when it slipped off the chair he had put it on. She did not feel we needed to be at Grandpa's funeral. She had made sure the funeral was over before we could get there and said the important people were there. Bill, Susan, and I were very hurt by not being allowed to attend the funeral. It still makes me sad when I think about it. We had gone to see him before his death, so we were able to say goodbye. Someone had given him a stuffed rabbit during his illness, and he gave it to Susan during our last visit. She still has it.

Tom lost his sobriety when his dad died after two and half years in AA. I later found out his father had told him how disappointed he was with Tom because he abused me and the children. Tom's anger at his dad and his drinking again caused the abuse to start to reappear. I found out later that my son Bill, now a man, had threatened his dad when we returned from Connecticut that if he ever hit me again, Bill would beat him up. The threat had helped for a while.

A few weeks later, I bought tickets for a play I wanted to see. Tom did not want to go and did not want me to go. I finally gave in and stayed home. A short time later, when it was too late for me to go, he decided to go out drinking and sleeping with hookers, which had been his usual weekend nighttime activity before he found AA. He always told me sleeping with hookers was not cheating, it was just business.

I blew up! I yelled at him, stormed into the bedroom, grabbed a suitcase, and started packing. When he came into the bedroom, I threw something at him. BIG MISTAKE! He grabbed me, started choking me, and threatened to break my neck. I am not sure why he stopped, but I did stop fighting. My fighting back was making him angrier and more violent. I knew it was best not to fight back when being abused. Tom was stronger than me, especially when he was angry. The better solution was to remove my children and myself to a safe place as quickly as possible. Nevertheless, I stayed . . . and hoped that he would go back to AA and reclaim the recovery he had found.

In April 1989 life again took an unexpected turn. As I walked down the stairs of the beautiful old historical building where I had worked for the past year and a half, I had to fight hard to keep from bursting into tears. My arms were full of all the personal items that made my office my home away from home. I had been laid off. How I hated the sound and reality of those words. I had an overwhelming sense of failure and betrayal. Why had I been laid off instead of someone else? In my heart, I knew the answer. This was God's will for my life. I had been unhappy in my job for months. I had been asked to falsify records and to keep an eye on my boss, whom the owner suspected of stealing. I found both situations very awkward. I refused to falsify records, so the other girl in my department did it. She was not laid off. Even though I was unhappy at my job, it still hurt. It felt like a knife had been plunged into my stomach.

The tears streamed down my face as I drove the twenty miles home. Luckily, my car seemed to know the way as I drove on automatic pilot. I just wanted to get home to my husband. I needed a hug and comfort. He had been laid off twice, so he would understand my pain. However, when I arrived home, instead of comfort, Tom met me with anger. "The layoff was your fault!" he shouted. His anger made the pain even worse. I did not know then that my job was not the only major loss I was to face in the next four months.

Tom's reaction to my layoff was another indication that my marriage of twenty years was in serious trouble again. After Tom's dad had died, instead of facing his grief, Tom had buried it. In the process, he had shut out our two children, God, and me. The more I hammered on the wall he had erected between us, the more withdrawn he became. What I did not know was that he had a girlfriend and was planning to leave us. My layoff was a glitch in his plans.

A few weeks later, Tom slammed the door to the den in my face. He had just told me he was leaving and then walked away. *This cannot be happening*, I thought. I had been trying so hard to make our marriage work. As I turned away from the door, I was overcome with anger. I pounded my fist into the wall. A small shelf of miniature silver plates fell and splattered all over the parquet floor, causing more noise than damage. Tom reappeared from the den long enough to say he had never seen such disgusting behavior. I stood there in total shock.

How could he say that my behavior was disgusting? I had put up with years of his abuse and cleaning up after his tantrums. Was this the same man who, in one of his rages, had opened the refrigerator and smashed all the jars inside, one by one, on the kitchen floor? Or what about the time he dumped my houseplants all over the living room furniture and carpet? Or the night he poured tea all over me at the dinner table? I stood there in disbelief that my one little hopeless punch into the wall in reaction to his leaving could be classified as "disgusting" by this monster. The following is a poem Susan wrote about another incident that happened when she was nine. It speaks volumes.

MONSTER IN DISGUISE

She flew across the room

A hand

A hand so big

It knocked the breath out of her

She hit the wall!

Her head began to throb

Tears made rivers down her cheeks

That was her only cry for help

The pain runs throughout her body

His temperature rises

Her hope lowers

His eyes are filled with a blaze of hatred

Words of hate run out of his mouth

He raises his hand again

However, lowers the towering hand slowly

He stares into the hallway blankly

He sees the young girl

She stares at him sadly

Her innocent eyes of blue turn gray

She viewed the horrible scene

She learned that night a valuable lesson

A person who looks sweet on the outside . . .

Can be a monster IN DISGUISE!

I went to bed alone, numb, and in shock. Tom moved out, taking all our money with him, including $700 of Girl Scout cookie money I had collected as the cookie chairperson for Susan's troop. The next two months were filled with tension and frustration. I was unable to find a job and became more and more desperate. I trusted that the layoff was God's plan, so I was sure He had a better job for me. I just needed to keep doing the legwork.

God provided a temporary job and I continued to interview for permanent positions. Then, after many dead-end leads, countless interviews, and depressing rejection letters, I was sure I had found the perfect job. The position matched my skills, salary requirements, and location needs perfectly. The boss and his assistants interviewed me for several hours over a two-day period. The company needed someone right away, and I was the only candidate. I was sure this was the job God had arranged for me.

I did not get the job. I asked, "Why?" I was just told I did not fit in. This latest loss sent me into a deep depression and a time of questioning God's will for my life. On top of that, Tom was also insisting I put our house up for sale. As if all these other losses were not enough to worry about, the doctor told me I needed both feet operated on. I was beginning to understand the Bible story of Job and how he must have felt when home, family, livelihood, and health were all taken away.

I went through the next few weeks doing what I had to do but feeling numb the entire time. Denial set in. I could not believe this was happening. Tom had filed for divorce.

He was taking care the paperwork and all the other details involved in separating our lives. My brother, Steve, had come to Houston to look for work and was staying with me for three weeks. His presence gave me a shoulder to cry on during this dark time.

Occasionally, flashes of anger would interrupt the denial and numbness. How could he leave me after I had tried so hard? I felt I had been a good wife. I had accepted his physical, emotional, sexual, and verbal abuse for twenty years. All through our marriage, I kept thinking if only I loved him enough, he would stop abusing me. I had always been there for him and our two children. So, how could he abandon Susan, my then twelve-year-old daughter, and me when I did not even have a job? How was I going to make ends meet? Bill, my son, was still in college and needed help. Where would the money come from for him to complete his education?

Then, my denial was broken. I attended a workshop sponsored by Al-Anon. I did not realize it was on using the twelve traditions of Alcoholics Anonymous to build good relationships, especially good marriages. I began to cry on Saturday afternoon and cried through most of the remaining workshop. That night when I got home, I continued to cry. I could not stop. I beat the bed and swore at God. Why had He brought me back to this marriage? I believed Tom had changed, so I came home from Connecticut. Why? Just so I could go through the pain of Tom leaving? And what about the message I got at the Marion Bond West workshop? That I would be a widow? At least then I would have money to live on.

I became more and more hysterical. My brother had gone back to Colorado. My daughter was away on a Girl Scout outing, so I was totally alone. I went through the five stages of grief[13] that night. First, denial that God could let this happen. Then, anger that it really was happening. I bargained with God to ease my pain. I felt utter hopelessness and depression, and I was overcome with feelings of being totally abandoned. After hours of crying, I was so exhausted! I just sat on the edge of my bed. A small book caught my eye. It was a volume[14] of specially selected Bible verses for times of need, which Tom had given me for Christmas. I began to read the book. One verse in particular stood out and seemed to answer my questions. Gradually a spirit of peace and love engulfed me, and I made it through the rest of the night.

The next morning, I went to church. As my priest started his sermon, he said that he was not going to preach on the assigned text for that day, but rather on the very verse that God had given me as comfort the night before. Romans 8:28 became my rock and anchor. Its promise, "And we know that God causes all things to work together for good to those who love God, to those who are called according to His purpose," continued to sustain me though many lonely nights and the tough days ahead.

A few days later, after I shared with my neighbor and friend my grief over not being able to find a job, she asked, "Did it

---

13   Defined by Elisabeth Kübler-Ross and David Kessler in their book, *On Grief and Grieving.* The five stages are a part of the framework that makes up our learning to live without the one we lost.

14   A. L. Gill, *God's Promises for Your Every Need* (Houston: J. Countryman, 1981).

ever occur to you that God might not want you to get a job? Maybe you're supposed to do something else."

"But what?" was my response. Susan was still at home with me. Bill needed help to complete his last two years of college. I needed a job!

She helped me realize that maybe I was to fulfill my lifelong dream of getting a college degree. I had been going to night school part time for two years and praying to go to school full time. She made me see that although I had been self-sufficient for twenty years, it was time to let go of my pride. A few days later, on Father's Day, 1989, I acted on faith and called my dad. After wishing him a happy Father's Day, I asked if he would help me get my college degree. His only response was, "Sure, how much do you need?"

Tears of joy ran down my face as I hung up the phone. God had answered my prayer to go to school full time. Finally, things were looking up even though I still experienced the stages of grief for several more months. Gradually I began to build a new life for myself. I let the feelings of anger and depression happen. I cried buckets of tears and walked miles to ease my anger. I went through all my feelings as they rose to the surface and then went on with my life one day at a time, as Al-Anon had taught me.

I have gained independence and self-reliance through many new and scary experiences. One such experience happened two months after Tom left me. My doctor told me I needed surgery on both my feet. Although I have had surgery many times before, Tom had always been there with me. This time

I would be alone. I was scared. I got up at 4:00 a.m. and drove myself to the hospital for the surgery. The road I took went through some bad areas of the city. I felt very afraid. Walking into the hospital all alone was hard. The nurses were nice and soon they gave me a shot to help me relax. As the medicine started taking effect, tears began to flow. I could not stop the tears. The doctor told me later that I cried all the way through surgery. When I awoke, I felt better than I had felt in months. All the tension caused by the separation, layoff, worry over money, and fear of the future had disappeared in those cleansing tears. This beautiful quote I found years later sums up the importance of tears.

Tears can be a life-giving signal for us in our lives, both individually and collectively. They can indicate that vital places within us that have become dormant are being stirred afresh. They can also be a type of washing of the inner lens. We have come to see certain things most clearly in our lives and relationships only through tears, the tears of pain and loss or the tears of delight and laughter . . . To pay attention to our tears is to hear the deepest longings of the human soul. It is to hear again the ancient yearning for well-being and harmony.[15]

My brother Steve and his fiancée picked me up and took me and my car home. I had made it through the surgery alone

---

15   Phillip J. Newell, *Christ of the Celts: The Healing of Creation* (San Francisco: Josey-Bass, 2008), xvii.

and felt better than when I went in. Maybe being single was going to be okay after all.

A few days later, July 4, 1989, came and went with tropical storm Allison. Both my feet were still bandaged, and I could barely walk. The rain caused the roof to leak, so I had to climb the stairs to the attic to put out buckets.

In terrible pain, I walked back to my chair in the living room to rest. As I stepped in the living room, I heard a squish under my feet. The wind had lifted the flashing around the chimney and rain was pouring down the wall and under the carpet. I started desperately trying to pull up the carpet while yelling for Susan to bring me towels. Amid the pain and chaos, the phone rang. It was Tom. He wanted to reconcile. I said I could not talk right then, and he yelled that if I did not decide then, we were done. God gave me the strength to calmly say, "Well, then, I guess we are done."

I hung up the phone and with a new strength went back to soaking up the water. I was surprised when he called because he had made a big deal about going out of town for the holiday with "friends." All I could figure was his girl-friend had dumped him, so he wanted to come home. With the strength God gave me, I did not let that happen. I was ready for a new life.

A few weeks later, after my feet were healed and the roof repaired, God and I started on my new life as a full-time college student. Three weeks later, my divorce was final. I gave Tom mostly all he asked for so I could be free of him. Material things were not as important as my freedom and peace.

I did not attend the proceedings. Since Tom had filed, I went to class that day. I remember telling a friend that I had only been miserable half the time my mother was. You see, my divorce was on my parents' forty-second wedding anniversary. I had been married twenty and a half years. Even though my dad was a wonderful man in many ways and respected in the community, always giving to others and providing leadership in many endeavors, he was a product of his generation and believed a woman's place was in the home waiting on him. He was not physically abusive or an alcoholic, but my mother once described him as "a dyed-in-the wool male chauvinist." He had many affairs throughout their marriage, which was painful for my mom and the source of her unhappiness. My mom had taught me by her example that you do not leave your husband just because he is unfaithful. Nevertheless, my mother was a woman ahead of her time. She liked to read and work outside the home, and as she said in a story she wrote in college, "My Fight to Live":

> I really wasn't dedicated to the idea of a cellar full of home canned foods or a closet full of handmade clothes . . . On the farm it was necessary for me to do many things such as baking my own bread, taking care of ninety dozen eggs a week . . . and feeding the harvest crews, but I never felt fully satisfied as a person doing them. Much of the time I lived in a state of anticipation, feeling that one day a great light would appear on the horizon to show me that I was doing the most fulfilling job possible . . . that light never appeared.

Then the opportunity for her to go to work came when my parents had three bad years on the farm, and Mom became a bookkeeper. She did that for twelve years, helping Dad become successful in his service station business. Even with a job, she was still resigned to her place in life:

> The idea of woman as a second class citizen, whose function was taking care of the male and bearing and rearing children, was firmly entrenched in my thinking. At times I would inwardly rebel against the situation but felt I was fighting the unchangeable laws of nature, so it was useless to struggle against my appointed role . . . For the most part I was satisfied to be a self-sacrificing martyr.

With Dad's success and us kids growing up, there came another time of change for my mom. Dad expected her to stay home and wait on him. She goes on to say in her story, "After two years of being bored stupid, sitting in my spotlessly clean, deadly quiet house, something had to change." Mom started making changes and fighting for her life. First, to her appearance: She lost weight, dyed her hair, and started getting her hair done each week. She said in her story that she no longer looked like a "dowdy, dumpy housewife." Then she decided to go to college. She enrolled in two college classes that interested her, English and History. Yes, she and I both shared the desire for higher education, to reach out and explore the world, and find who we were in our own right. And yes, we both had struggles with our husbands.

But our lives went in different directions. Mom stayed married and eventually gave up the fight after two years of attending college classes, but at least she knew she could do it. She got A's in all her classes. I got divorced and obtained my degree.

My mom was a good wife to my dad and a good mom to the five of us, just like I tried to be to my family. Her fortitude and dedication to her marriage, even living a life that was expected of her generation, had a strong influence on me trying to save my first marriage and staying as long as I did. I have always felt she died at sixty-four to set Dad free to find a wife who could meet his needs and so he would not have to take care of her as her health continued to decline.

Twenty-five years after my mom died as I was writing this book, I felt a strong nudge to read the story she wrote in college. Dad had sent me all her college papers many years earlier, but I had never read them. Even though I had known on some level she was unhappy, I cried with a broken heart to read in her own words about her feelings of being bored and unfulfilled and struggling to find herself. I also cried for our lost relationship. I had always felt she was ashamed of me for getting pregnant in college. Now I know she was not ashamed of me. She was disappointed and sad that I was losing my chance to develop into the person I wanted to be. She saw the ramifications of my pregnancy for my future in a much clearer light than I did.

Because of my shame and pride, our few conversations as adults were strained. I felt she did not understand my situation and we never talked about it. Her story helped me to see that she did understand my struggles, and I now know now that she celebrated in her quiet way my eventual freedom to become ME! I still miss her and my dad, who died twenty years after my mom. And yes, he did find a younger, healthier wife just as Mom had hoped. Lila was a nurse and took good care of him until he died and went to join my mom.

CHAPTER SIX

RISING FROM THE ASHES

"*There is an appointed time for everything,* and a time for every affair under the heavens . . . a time to heal . . . a time to build. A time to weep, and a time to laugh; a time to mourn, and a time to dance." Ecclesiastes 3: 1, 3–4.

It is time for my recovery and for me to rise from the ashes. It is time to build a new life, to be restored. It is time to let God heal my broken heart and set me on a healthy path. I need to travel a path where I am attracted to men who are NOT abusive. I do not want to repeat the same mistake again. It is time for me to "Arise, shake off the dust, sit enthroned . . . Loose the bonds from your neck, captive daughter," as it commands in Isaiah 52:2.

By the time my divorce was final, I had learned to balance my checkbook, handle my meager finances, and arranged repairs on my car and house. I was now a full-time college student and making it. I was becoming my own person, someone I liked. My anger had subsided, but my depression continued.

I reached out to a twelve-step program again. I needed to deal with my weight; I had always been heavy.

Maybe Overeaters Anonymous (OA)[16] would help me to get my weight under control, I thought. Here are some of my diary entries during that time that reflect the struggles I was going through.

Dear God, I feel hopeful and excited but a little afraid at giving up my food. Food has a hold on me. What will happen if I break that hold and surrender my life to you? I only want you to have a hold on me, not food or anything else. You are my God. My life. My love. Thank you for taking this burden from me. Love, Kathy

Dear God, Forgive me for being my own worst enemy. For not coming to you each day. For letting worry and fear rule my life. For eating for comfort and strength when I should come to you for courage and strength. Heal my eating, Lord, and give me strength to spend time with you each day. I need a spiritual director. Help me, Lord, find a spiritual director today. Love, Kathy

Dear God, I am powerless over the [piles of] mail and filing and this house [is out of control!]. Help me get it in order so I will have more peace in my life. I am powerless over my healing. I am powerless over my eating. Help me God. I am

---

16 Overeaters Anonymous is a fellowship of individuals who, through shared experience, strength, and hope, are recovering from compulsive overeating.

powerless over my part-time job and school. I give everything to you for you to guide me to your way. What do you want me to do? Thank you, God, for taking charge of my life and guiding me every day in every way. Amen.

Dear God, Am I over-concerned about externals? I worry about my children. I do not want them to hurt. I want their lives and their children's lives to be good. I know I need to let them go. Help me Lord. I am tired. Amen.

I continued with OA for some time, and it gave me insights into my eating and my inner self. I still felt sad most of the time, but I put on a happy face and went on each day. I had a vision for my life. After I obtained my present goal of an accounting degree and CPA's license, I wanted to go to law school to become a divorce attorney. I dreamed that these two degrees would help me handle both the financial and legal aspects of divorce so I could help others survive the trauma of divorce and rebuild their lives. I did not know where I would get the money for law school, but I continued to trust my life to God. [My dream of law school never happened, but this book is a fulfillment of my dream to help others. God has put many turns in my journey over the years, leading me in a different direction than where I thought I was going, but still honoring my dreams to serve others through Him.]

I found that participating in therapy, grief support groups, conferences, retreats, spiritual direction, and other programs such as Overeaters Anonymous and Al-Anon helped in my healing process. In addition, I found writing in a journal or on any handy scrap of paper how I felt, helped. I reached out beyond my church to find grief support groups and help. I have shared my stories of my growth in these programs to illustrate some ways to recover and the type of groups that might help you, my reader.

The importance of healing and reaching out is illustrated in the story my good friend, Millie, recently shared with me. She had jumped from her divorce into another marriage without any healing. She just stuffed the first man who came along into the hole left in her heart. God told her not to marry this man, who was handsome and charming, but she was being rebellious and did it anyway. She was beaten so badly each time she became pregnant, she miscarried three times. She almost lost her life on several occasions. God told a friend of Millie's that if the she did not convince Millie to get out of her marriage, Millie's blood would be on her hands. As her friend was telling Millie what God had told her, another woman came up to them and with a look of authority on her face, pointed her finger at Millie, and said, "You must listen to what she is telling you. Your life depends on it!" Then the woman walked away and disappeared. Millie and her friend believed the woman was an angel who wanted to be sure that Millie took her need to escape seriously.

Millie immediately went home, left the outside doors open, walked to the bedroom, and packed a small bag. She did not speak to her husband who was drinking in the living room. She then walked straight out the open doors and was able to get into her car and escape before her husband realized what was happening. She went to her friend's home and hid for several months. Her friend helped her get a divorce and gave her moral support until Millie was strong enough to live on her own. Her husband made a few phone calls to try and get her back, but she resisted his charm. Eventually he moved out of state and died three years later from alcoholism. Millie has healed and developed a deep faith in God through Bible studies, grief groups, self-help books, and loving friends.

Often, having someone else intervene is the only way an abused woman gets out alive. Sometimes abused women do not know they have the resources or self-esteem to get out and make on it on their own. I know that was true of me for a long time. My abuser had made me believe I was not capable of taking care of myself and my children. He was wrong, and so are other abusers. There are agencies and people willing to help.

After I got out of my marriage, I knew I needed to heal. I did not want to repeat the same mistake of marrying an abusive person again. I needed to recover for Bill and Susan too. Two of my most painful regrets are staying too long in my abusive marriage and the damage my staying caused to my children. Sometimes people say you should stay together for the children's sake, but that is not true in an abusive situation. I found that in most cases of abuse, the sooner you get out, find help, and recover, the better off your children will be.

Some of my friends said I made recovery a full-time job. Besides attending many grief programs, I wrote stories for *New*

Perspectives.[17] I gave several talks and facilitated discussions as part of the teams for several recovery programs. I have left some of my stories and talks intact here because they clearly reflect how I felt at the time. I hope that if some of you are going through the loss of a spouse by death or divorce, these stories might help you reach out and find help.

The following story shows how I learned to deal with being alone on holidays and at other times.

MY FIRST THANKSGIVING

My first Thanksgiving alone was less than two months after my divorce. My daughter was at her father's and my son was with his fiancée. We had always lived far from family, so holidays had meant just the four of us. Now everyone was somewhere else!

Thanksgiving has always been my favorite holiday. It doesn't have all the pressures of gift-giving that come with Christmas. I love to cook and fix turkey with all the trimmings. So I decided to make my first Thanksgiving as a single woman special.

I invited a few friends who were also alone and my brother Steve, who had just moved to Houston. They all brought others they knew were alone. We ended up with ten of us for dinner. My friends brought their eight-year-old daughter, and she helped me decorate a "Thanksgiving Box." Everyone was given several small pieces of paper and told to write down one thing they were thankful for on each piece of paper and put it in the box.

---

17 *New Perspectives* was the newsletter for the divorced, separated, and widowed. See the Programs Attended resource page at the end of the book for more information.

After dinner, we opened the box and read them as a group. It was great! We all had so much to be thankful for and sharing it aloud with friends was even better. But best of all, there was no time for loneliness or self-pity!

That Thanksgiving taught me several things. First, how to open my heart and my home to others. In so doing, I received more than I gave.

Second, I have choices. I could have chosen to feel sorry for myself and sat home alone. Instead, I made plans and took risks. Lastly, new traditions can be fun and create beautiful memories. Our "Thanksgiving Box" has become a special memory.

As I mentioned earlier, denial is one of the five stages in the grieving process along with anger, bargaining, depression, and acceptance. Denial can be very powerful and almost prevented me from continuing to heal. This next story tells how I followed others' recommendations to start breaking though my denial and continued my recovery, even after I thought I was done.

Through The Journey[18] program and four very special women, God led me to RSVP.[19] He knew I needed the program's healing magic and was not finished with my grieving. I had an overwhelming sense that God was starting me on a special journey to prepare me for His purpose. RSVP was the

---

18   The Journey Program was a quarterly program to help divorced and widowed persons. See Programs Attended resource page at the end of the book for more information.

19   Response Support for Valuable People (RSVP): A support program for the recently separated, divorced, or widowed that met for ten successive weeks. See Programs Attended resource page at the end of the book for more information.

first step. Being a participant and later serving as a facilitator were both tremendous growth experiences.

WELCOME TO RSVP

As my school friend and I entered the Cameron Retreat Center[20] *that first night, I was a little apprehensive as to what was going to happen. Several people greeted me warmly and said they were glad I was there. Although they seemed very sure about it, I was not so sure I belonged there. After registration, I found a seat in the big room. The first thing I noticed was all the Kleenex boxes around the room. Were these people expecting me to cry? I had been beyond that point for some time.*

In fact, I did not feel like this program would help me at all, but I would try to listen with an open mind—at least for this session. After the opening ceremonies, the team members began sharing their losses, and the little voice inside my head began to chatter. What am I doing here? I do not need this! I should be home studying. I have a test tomorrow and need to study. Being a full-time student at the University of Houston is all I can handle right now. As these thoughts ran through my head, I began to listen to the speaker. Some of what she said made sense and sounded okay. However, my resentment at being there deepened with each passing moment. My thoughts began to drift again. I spent last summer working on my grief. I was going on with my new life. I did not need or want to look back anymore.

---

20 Cameron Retreat Center is owned by the Archdiocese of Galveston-Houston St. Dominic's Center. Retreats are given there for engaged couples, married couples, singles, and other groups.

When it came time to write and reflect on what I heard, I wrote, "Why am I here? I am doing okay. My pain is getting less. I am going on with life. I am free to be me! At last!" More thoughts accompanied this last statement. Yes, free at last! I had wanted out of my marriage even before Tom and I got married. I had married out of fear—terrible, all-encompassing terror of Tom—and out of weakness, not love. The battering had begun even before we were married. I had stayed because of fear and intense pride. I was too proud to admit to my family or anyone I had made a mistake. Now here I am, finally—free, after twenty years of being trapped. I want to celebrate, not grieve my divorce. Why do people keep saying I must grieve? And why do these sad, nagging feelings of depression keep popping up when I least expect them? I do not want to feel any more pain. I want to go on with my life. I went back to school to fulfill a lifetime dream of getting a college degree. I have made friends and gotten involved in new activities. I am dating and having fun whenever possible. Still, the nagging feelings of pain and loneliness keep coming back.

The speaker shared her experience of being divorced and single. I do not like being called divorced or single. I would have preferred to be a "widow." It sounds better. I felt that "widow" did not have the stigma attached that the term divorced has. I had never planned on being divorced. I always thought Tom would die and leave me a widow. That was what God told me at the Marion Bond West program years earlier. A friend helped me to understand the message. She shared the scripture verse I Corinthians 7:15 which states: "If the unbeliever separates, however, let him separate. The brother or sister is not bound in such cases; God has called you to peace." Tom was a non-believer, so, yes, in God's eyes I am a widow even if it is through divorce.

So here I am, divorced and going on. But, why did I come to RSVP? To be honest, I do know why I came. I had gotten a very clear message through several people that this was something God wanted me to do. In January, I had attended The Journey Program. I ran into an old friend I had not seen for some time. She saved me from a lonely supper by asking me to join her and her companions for dinner. She had just completed RSVP, and her companions were all facilitators in the program. They encouraged me to come to RSVP, but I had serious doubts about committing the time. I also was not convinced I needed the program. I prayed about it. I asked God to send someone to carpool with me if He really wanted me to attend.

Three days later, I casually mentioned RSVP to a newly divorced school friend. She immediately said she would like to go with me. I was so surprised at her immediate response. I knew it was another message from God and that I had to go. Still, why did God think I needed RSVP? I really needed to be concentrating on my schoolwork, and after all, I thought I was okay. I already had a good support group and three and one-half years of recovery in Al-Anon behind me. I had worked hard at recovery even before my divorce, at feeling my feelings, at coping with life. What was I going to learn here? These people around me are in such pain, I thought to myself. I can see it in their faces and hear it in their voices. How are they going to help me when they need so much help themselves?

As these thoughts continued to race around my head, I grew more angry and resentful. I was surprised at how intensely angry I got when a member of my group shared that she was past her need to share her story. Her pain was so visible. I needed to hear her story and understand her pain, and now I actually felt cheated. It was becoming clear to me that my real reason for being there was to listen to others, learn from their experience, and absorb some of their strength. I paused and thought, Hmmm . . . maybe I do need to be here.

After our small group sharing, I met up with my friend again. She was so excited about the program and was positive it was going to help her. I began to realize that my reaction was a problem with me, not the program. Anger is not an emotion I am comfortable with, so for the next few days following the first session, I wrote and explored why I was feeling so angry. I discovered that my anger came from my own denial of the grieving I still needed to face—grief from feelings I had stuffed and covered up. However, even with this realization, I debated whether or not to go back. I felt bad leaving Susan home at night and I did need to study. I was not sure I could afford the time.

In the end, I did decide to go to the second session, if for no other reason than I knew it was God's will for me. After all, He had sent three people to tell me about RSVP and a friend to carpool with to the sessions. I have found that when I am faithful to His will, things go better. God always seems to know what is best for me. Romans chapter 8, verse 28 was still my rock in the storm of uncertainty and confusion since Tom left, and I continued to believe its promise: "All things work together for good to them that love God, to them who are the called according to His purpose." And maybe, down deep inside, I knew I really needed RSVP.

I found peace and acceptance at the second session. I had not realized that turbulent first night the blessings RSVP had in store for me. RSVP worked its magic on me, just as it has on others before me. I did not realize I was burying an overwhelming sense of failure under my well-adjusted exterior, or that I was acting "wifely" in a new relationship to prove I could succeed at being a wife. I was trying to prove that Tom was wrong to have left me—to prove I was not a failure. RSVP in ten short weeks turned my life upside down. I was released from the terrible anger I still felt toward Tom; RSVP helped me to realize the anger came from my feelings of failure. I had tried so hard to make my marriage work. I had given over twenty years to it. Thanks to RSVP, I have been able to look at the good things that came out of my marriage. Two of the best things in my life are my children, Bill and Susan, who have richly blessed my life. I have grown from a naïve teenager to a mature woman. I have learned many new skills and how to be self-sufficient. I have even come to appreciate having a Kleenex box close by.

The members of my small group helped me so much. I think back to one special woman who, in her quiet way, challenged me to look deeper into myself. Another member inspired all of us in the spunky way she grabbed recovery with gusto and worked at overcoming her grief as though it was a full-time job. I am also grateful to all the men in my small group and on the team who taught me that men could be caring, gentle people, who feel as much pain at the loss of a spouse as women do. The love these special men showed for their children, and the pain they suffered at not being a daily part of their children's lives, gave me a new perspective on my own situation. Their sharing helped me see that my ex-husband was also in pain and needed to be treated with respect and dignity. Then there were all the special people on the team who gave unselfishly of their time and energy, offering stories of loss to pass on the RSVP magic to others. Our team leader was an inspiration and model of recovery for me. Her wit, insight, and devotion added much to my RSVP experience.

I continued to learn more lessons that helped me heal and lead a joyful life, as the next story shows.

A TIME TO PLAY

I asked my school friend one day, "Have you ever snapped a snapdragon?" We had a long break before our next class at the University of Houston, where we were both students, and it was a beautiful day. She asked me, "What's a snapdragon?" With that question, we were on our way across campus to a beautiful batch of yellow, pink, and orange snapdragons in front of the U of H library. We sat in the middle of the flowers laughing for over thirty minutes while I taught her the art of snapping a snapdragon.

My great-grandfather taught me how to snap the snapdragons in his backyard when I would go stay with him. Snapdragons are flowers, which have two parts closed together. When pinched gently on the sides, the parts open like a "mouth." Of course, part of the fun is to make up a conversation as the mouth opens and closes. If done properly, the flower is not hurt.

As my fortieth birthday and the one-year anniversary of my husband of twenty years walking out on me approached, I decided to begin "playing" again, and letting the little child inside of me have fun. I printed flyers for a fortieth birthday party on pink paper and entitled the party, "Life Begins at Forty." All the decorations were pink, and everyone was instructed NOT to bring "black" gifts. I was being reborn, not dying!

My favorite gift now sits on my piano. It was a beautiful kaleidoscope, something I played with at my grandma's house and had always wanted as a child. Often "Little Kathy" picks it up and looks at the beautiful colors and designs that are constantly changing as it turns. A colorful example of my life.

"Little Kathy" has become a wonderful part of my life. "Cookies, cookies, cookies!" I hollered one evening in my little girl voice. My daughter Susan started laughing. "'Little Kathy's' out, Mom," she replied. "Yes, and she wants cookies," I said. We continued the "little girl dialogue," with Susan playing "Little Susie" to my "Little Kathy" while we made cookies. It was great fun, and what "child" does not love warm chocolate chip cookies fresh out of the oven? Playing has brought Susan and me closer together and relieved many tense situations. When the strain of being a single parent gets too much, or Susan gets mad at me for some oversight or mistake (moms are not perfect!), "Little Kathy" will stick out her lip and make some crazy comment. The tension is lessened, the lines

of communication are opened, and we usually both end up laughing. Susan has begun to let "Little Susie" out to play more and more. When she is feeling tired or hurt, needing a little extra mothering, she uses "Little Susie" to ask for a back rub or extra hug. After all, a "grown-up" teenager could not admit to still needing mom!

But the truth of the matter is each of us has a wonderful child inside who enjoys the freshness and newness of life, a special child who laughs, plays, and does not worry about image or adult rules of behavior. A little child who loves unconditionally and accepts life as an adventure. Is it time you let your little child out to play? Remember your childhood and something you really enjoyed, such as flying a kite, splashing in a puddle, sitting in the surf, whatever. Try it! It is fun and very healing. I am glad I found the time to play and look forward to many more years of fun and laughter to come.

Almost one year from the night I cried my heart out, I attended a Catholic Beginning Experience (BE).[21] After completing RSVP, I felt I had worked through my grief, and that I would not benefit from BE. I was wrong, just as I had been about RSVP. My Beginning Experience weekend was an intense growth opportunity. It took me deeper into myself than I had ever been. The team's sharing of their losses, the questions I answered, and the small group sharing were all powerful. On Sunday morning, I began to cry. I cried for over an hour before

---

21   Beginning Experience (BE) is a weekend retreat to help put closure on a relationship. See Programs Attended resource page at the end of the book for more information.

I was able to stop. I realized that I had not completely let go of Tom. I still had a thread of hope that our relationship would be restored. Admitting it was over hurt. Beginning Experience helped me let go of my hope and truly grieve the end of my marriage. Without this final step of letting go, I could never fully go on with my new life.

At the Beginning Experience weekend, although I was not Catholic, I went to talk to the priest. I freed myself of my guilt over my failed marriage and an earlier flirtation. Later I wrote a goodbye letter to Tom and forgave him for the years of abuse. I asked for his forgiveness for my part in the breakdown of our marriage. I even wrote a thank-you note to my former boss who had laid me off and thanked him for setting my life in a new direction. I had thought I was healed! I was wrong, and the process of recovery continued.

After my ten-week session in RSVP, I was asked to be a facilitator. Serving as a facilitator gave me more time to process my own grief, and writing talks on my loss gave me the opportunity to look deeper into myself. Here is another story of how I saw the healing that was happening from my perspective as a team member. It was published in *New Perspectives* and reflects how grief groups and the support of others lead us to healing.

RSVP'S GIFT OF HEALING

It is time for a new session of RSVP to start. As I stand by the door and watch each new participant approach, I see the tension and pain in their faces. There is apprehension in their walk: slow, deliberate steps. As I open the door and greet them, many sigh with relief to know they are in the right place. Others want to hurry on down the hall to the registration table and get on with it. I remember the night that I first walked up that sidewalk. I was apprehensive about what was going to happen. It took courage to reach out for help.

After being greeted warmly by the team members, most people find their way into the meeting room and sit quietly. There are few smiles and little talking before the session begins. Nervous side-glances at each other are exchanged. Again, as I watch these new participants, I remember my first night as I, too, looked around and tried to figure out why these people were here. I remember thinking that everyone seemed very under control. But despite their efforts to hide their feelings, the pain came through. Was my pain also showing? As this session begins, I see people gradually become aware, just as I did on my first night, that everyone in the room has been through the same pain they are experiencing, just with different circumstances.

The tension gradually starts to subside. The participants slowly start to realize through the talks that the team has also walked the same path of loss. Now we want to reach back and help these new fellow travelers along, and in the process, continue our own journey. Loss through divorce or death of a spouse has brought us all, participants and team members, together with a common bond. As the evening progresses, slowly, ever so slowly, the special RSVP magic begins to take over. The healing process has begun.

After the writing and reflection time, it is time for the small groups. We sit here now as strangers, but I know that will change. I remember the special people in my group when I was a participant. We also began as strangers, but through the wonderful magic of RSVP, we became loving, caring friends, developing a closeness that sharing our common pain can bring. I am excited to watch that process begin tonight with these new participants.

As we disband and the first evening ends, the bonding process is already well under way. People are talking quietly to a new friend they have found. There is still some tension, but the barriers between people have begun to come down.

The second night starts with the participants greeting the few people and team members they met the week before. It took courage to come back, to feel the pain, to be vulnerable by sharing your story. The fragile bonds made the previous week are being strengthened. The talk is still quiet and reserved, but laughter is beginning to pop up here and there. By the end of the small group sharing time, the level of talking has greatly increased. Hugs, laughter, tears, and caring are filling the room. The bonding process is off the ground and healing is taking place. I remember my own experience as a participant. I felt so much better as I left that second session. I really felt that I belonged here and that these people cared about me. It was a warm, wonderful feeling.

As the third session begins, participants are greeting each other as friends. More sharing and caring are flowing tonight. Feelings are being felt and healing is continuing to happen. The growing trust in the other participants, in the team members, and in the process is evident throughout the room. It is beautiful to watch and be a part of the process. As the evening ends, the team leader is having difficulty getting everyone to quiet down for the closing announcements. How this group has changed! The bonding process has almost totally taken place now.

Utter bedlam greets the team leader as she tries to close the fourth session. Talking, sharing, and hugging mixed with tears and laughter fills the room. It is beautiful to see how in four short weeks, all these strangers in pain have reached out and become caring friends. The bonding process is complete. The next six sessions will build on these bonds and healing will continue. By the tenth session, the participants will have made lasting friendships, and be well down the road to a happier, fuller life.

As we gather for the tenth session, a certain sadness and sense of completion fills the air. Plans are made to keep in touch and tears are shed over the session ending. I know that even if we never see some of these people again, a special place exists in each of our hearts for the other participants and team members. A special memory has been created, a bond that will never break. This bond has helped the healing process move forward in each of us, participants and team members alike. RSVP, like many of the other self-help programs, is a truly beautiful, magical experience of caring and sharing. The program brings the gift of healing to all it touches through the bonding process and the sharing of our stories.

After my divorce, my feelings of loneliness made me dislike being at home, especially if my daughter was gone. Too many bad memories. My husband's suicide attempt, the beatings, and other painful memories plagued me when I was home. A year after my divorce, I had my house blessed. What a difference that made! God cleaned my house and my spirit. Since then, it has become a haven for me, a happy, peaceful place. I enjoy the solitude I find there. The house and furnishings are still very much the same, but I have changed. With this change, and through the many self-help programs I have attended, has come a different perspective on life. I have stopped retreating from myself. I have gotten to know me. I now use the solitude of my home to renew my spirit and be with me.

This new life of mine is becoming happy, joyous, and free. I have hope for the future. My self-esteem has improved with each new task I undertake. That next summer was so different from the one before. I had felt my life had been in ashes, and now I have risen out of them with a completely new life.

Instead of tears, loneliness, and depression, my life is filled with the beauty that comes from the ashes, with laughter, friends, and happiness. I am happier than I have ever been. I have grown into a self-sufficient woman whom I like, but who still knows the importance of just being held in God's hands. I realize that life is a journey that I will never complete. I have more growth ahead of me. I can truly say that my divorce was an important catalyst for growth in my life. Here is an article I wrote for *New Perspectives* about finding joy amid the growth.

IN RECOVERY GOD'S FLOWERS BLOOM
It is through recovery that God's flowers bloom in our lives. Here is how I felt as I approach the one-year anniversary

of my divorce and my four-year birthday in Al-Anon. I feel like a flower that is opening, petal by petal. My last four years in recovery have consisted of hard work, work which started with planting the seed of trust in God. Work which continued with weeding my life of all my character defects, one by one as they popped up to the surface. Some character defects continue to crop up, and I must be forever vigilant in keeping my life free of them, so I can continue to grow. The grief support groups and weekend programs, many twelve-step meetings, therapy sessions, spiritual workshops, miracles, and prayers have served as fertilizer for my seed of trust. God has sent rain, rivers of tears. He sent the sunshine, the love and care of many friends, and a loving family to help with the growth.

Slowly, very slowly, the beautiful flower of my life is opening and enjoying both the warmth of the sunshine and the healing of the rain. I know weeds will continue to spring up now and then. There will be rainy days mixed in with sunny ones. However, my roots are now firmly planted in God's love. As all plants do, I am continuing daily to reach upwards toward the sky and God's promise of a happy, joyous, and free life, lived according to His plan for me. Through the process of recovery, my small seed of trust has bloomed into a beautiful flower of joy.

Many books also helped me in my healing. After becoming a member of the staff of *New Perspectives*, I wrote book reviews. Here is one of those reviews:

CLIMBING THE MOUNTAIN TO FREEDOM

The following poem begins chapter four entitled "Guilt vs. Rejection: Dumpers 1, Dumpees 0" of Rebuilding: When Your Relationship Ends, *by Bruce Fisher, Ed.D.*

I laughed so hard . . .

It was the funniest joke I ever heard;

"He doesn't love you."

And it was even funnier

When you told it yourself;

"I don't love you."

And I laughed so hard

That the whole house shook,

And came crashing down upon me.

This wonderful paperback book Rebuilding: When Your Relationship Ends *is a step-by-step guide to recovery from the grief caused by the ending of a love relationship. As the above poem illustrates, this book has empathy and understanding of the pain caused by ending relationships. Many people who have ended a love relationship, either through death or divorce, have felt their world "crashing down" on them.*

However, the book has far more than just understanding. It also has helpful, easy-to-follow steps to healthy living and better future relationships. Dr. Fisher feels that there is "an adjustment process—with a beginning, an end, and specific steps of learning along the way" to recover from the loss of a relationship. Each chapter in the book starts with what Dr.

Fisher calls a rebuilding block. The first chapter starts with denial and the book continues through anger, letting go, love, trust, sexuality, and many more stages until a person reaches the top "rebuilding block of freedom."

At the end of each chapter is a checklist to help identify and check progress along the way. Some of the items from the checklist at the end of the chapter three, which is entitled "From Loneliness to Aloneness," are:

1. I have stopped running from loneliness.

2. I have begun to fill up my time with activities important to me.

3. I have stopped trying to find another love relationship just to avoid being lonely.

4. I am not letting the feelings of loneliness control my behavior.

This is not a book to read and put on the shelf. It is a book to be read and reread, chapter by chapter, as a person proceeds through the grieving process. The final chapter ends with a self-evaluation report card that can be used every month or two to evaluate overall progress and identify areas that may still need growth.

Dr. Fisher sums up his last chapter, which is on freedom, by asking, "What is the freedom we all seem to be striving for?" He answers his own question this way: "Freedom is something you *find inside you. And you find it by becoming free from unmet needs which control you, such as the need to avoid being alone, the need to feel guilty, the need to find a critical parent to please, or the need to get free from your own 'parent within you.'" His book is certainly a good way to start on the climb up the mountain of grief to the goal of inner freedom and future happiness.*

I was so blessed to have so many programs to attend during my healing process. This article from *New Perspectives* is about the first Arise and Walk Conference[22] I attended and all the nuggets of wisdom I learned.

HEALING STRONGER IN THE BROKEN PLACES

Attending the Arise and Walk Conference in March 1991 was another stop along the way in my recovery. From the opening speaker, Antoinette Bosco, to the dance on Saturday night, the tenth annual Arise and Walk Conference was for me an experience of healing, growth, and fellowship. I attended with 350 other participants who filled the St. Francis de Sales Catholic Church's facilities in Houston, Texas.

In keeping with the conference theme of "Be Not Afraid," Ms. Bosco inspired me to "go beyond my limits to heal." Her wit, humor, and courage left me with a new spirit of determination. She encouraged me to grow through my pain by quoting Hemingway: "The world breaks all of us; some of us heal stronger in the broken places." The idea behind Hemingway's words is

22 The Arise and Walk Conference was an annual conference for the widowed and divorced. See Programs Attended resource page at the end of the book for more information.

that where a bone has been broken and then heals, the break becomes the strongest part of the bone. The same is true of our broken places. When we bring Christ into the places where we have been hurt, fallen, or failed, we become stronger. His strength and healing is made perfect in and through our weaknesses. This has stuck with me and continues to be a thought I share with others who are going through a tough time. [In fact, it inspired me to write this book.]

Ms. Bosco shared that ministering to other people helps all of us heal. Our friends are not helped so much by our brilliant logic or persuasive speech, as they are through honest sharing of our own struggles and how, with God's help, we have overcome.

Ms. Bosco continued by saying that our faith in Christ is just a case of one beggar showing another beggar where to find bread. God, of course, does not want us to stay stuck in our sins and problems. While God loves and accepts us as we are, and uses us as we are, he loves us too much to leave us as we are. But never think that you have too little talent or too many hurts or problems for God to use you. "[God] said to me [Paul], 'My grace is sufficient for you, for power is made perfect in weakness.' I will rather boast most gladly of my weaknesses, in order that the power of Christ power may dwell with me." II Corinthians 12:9.

Ms. Bosco helped me when she explained that many of the men and women in the Bible, who were used by God, had personal struggles or challenges of one kind or another. Moses stuttered. John Mark was rejected by Paul. Timothy had ulcers. Hosea's wife was a prostitute. Amos' only training was in the school of fig-tree pruning. Jacob lied. David had an affair.

Solomon had too many wives and concubines. Jesus was too poor and was not schooled in the right religious institutions. Abraham and Sarah were too old. David was too young. Peter was impulsive. John had a temper. Naomi was a widow. Paul was a murderer, as was Moses. Jonah ran from God. Gideon and Thomas both doubted. Jeremiah was depressed. Elijah was burned out. Martha worried too much. Matthew was a despised tax-gatherer. Noah had a drinking problem.

The key issue is to be available and willing like the Virgin Mary when the angel appeared to her. In Luke 1:38, "Mary said, 'Behold, I am the handmaid of the Lord. May it be done to me according to your word.'" Everyone that God has ever used has had his or her weaknesses, sins, and failings. Nevertheless, they were available and willing. They have been remembered for what God did through their lives. I trust God will do the same for me as I make myself available and willing for Him to use every day. My prayer continues to be: Dear God, I am available and willing. Use me today to be like Jesus to every life I touch. Thank you for hearing and answering my prayer. In Jesus' name, Amen.

Saturday also started on a very upbeat note with Tony Granelli, whose dream inspired the Arise and Walk Conference. He gave the story of the first conference ten years ago, which started with a lot of faith inside and pickets outside. After all, they were ministering to divorced people in a Catholic Church. A new idea. Awesome how far the Church has come in reaching out to those who are hurting.

Tony introduced Virginia Clemente, who gave the keynote address entitled, "I Am Not Afraid but Hold Me While I'm

Learning to Let Go." Ms. Clemente imparted what she had learned about the importance of the healing process and forgiveness. As Ms. Clemente said, "What we do not heal, we will repeat; what we repeat, we'll pass on." It is important to heal, not just for the person experiencing the pain, but also for their children. Ms. Clemente explained the stages of denial that often bring on divorce, and the needed steps to recovery. She closed by saying, "Love is a gift, but it is not a gift until it is shared or given away."

I attended Virginia Clemente's workshop entitled "Love—Will I Recognize It When It Happens?" She went through the stages of falling in love and gave very practical advice on how to have a healthy love relationship. She ended with an inspirational quote on the value of growing and risking from Mother Teresa: "God never asks us to be successful, God just asks us to try."

Shortly after the Arise and Walk Conference, a friend was killed by her estranged husband and abuser in a double murder-suicide. She belonged to my Daughters of the King prayer group. She had prayed for me and I had prayed for her. We had both been going through the same types of trials with alcoholic, violent husbands and the pain of divorce. As I sat at her funeral, I wondered at God's grace. It could have been me in her place. Why was I spared, and she was not? "God, where are we going on this road of life?" I asked. I felt I had to live my life for both of us. I felt like I needed to repay God for sparing me and to make up for her dying too early at the age of fifty-three.

The end of April, Elizabeth Harper Neeld, PhD, was the speaker at The Journey Program. She shared the major stages of grief from her book[23] while sharing her personal story of loss and the stories of others. The stage that spoke to me that day was reconstruction. Dr. Neeld said, "Reconstruction means making painful but beneficial changes. Working to establish a new identity appropriate to present circumstances . . . Many people mistakenly equate mourning only with early acute grief signals like crying, pining, and being depressed. But mourning also includes remaking ourselves and building a new structure for our lives."

I am restructuring my life by working toward completing my education, attending and facilitating grief support groups, and learning to live as a whole single person. I have grown into the stage of acceptance most of the time. Occasionally anger or depression comes back, but for a shorter time, and with less pain than before. My feelings today are summed up on the last page of a beautiful little book called *How to Survive the Loss of a Love*[24] by Melba Colgrove, PhD, Harold H. Bloomfield, MD, and Peter McWilliams.

❀ I loved, which was purgatory.

❀ I lost, which was hell.

❀ And I survived. Heaven!

---

23   Elizabeth Harper Neeld, PhD. *Seven Choices: Finding Daylight After Loss Shatters Your World* (New York: Warner Books, 1990).

24   Melba Colgrove, PhD, Harold H. Bloomfield, MD, and Peter McWilliams, *How to Survive the Loss of a Love* (Allen Park, MI: Prelude Press, 2000).

While I was working hard on my recovery, school life continued. The next story is how I took a risk with my new self-esteem, experienced hurt, and eventually experienced even better things than I could have imagined.

RISKING: IT IS WORTH IT!

They are laughing at me! Why was I so stupid to think a forty-year-old woman could come back to college and be elected vice president of a fraternity? Was this a risk or just stupidity? Was I trying to recapture my youth, or did I really have a right to hold an office? These and many more questions pounded through my head as I cried and beat myself up verbally all the way home from the University of Houston that night.

A few members of Beta Alpha Psi, the accounting honors fraternity, had encouraged me to run for vice president. I was told I needed to prepare a speech. I wrote a speech, outlining my accomplishments in other organizations such as my Civic Club and the PTA. When I started to give my speech, I was so scared my voice was shaking. As I stated each accomplishment, it was met with snickers and laughter from a group of young men on the front row. The more they snickered, the more I stumbled over my words and lost my composure. A formal speech was not what they expected or wanted. I lost the election.

However, what was worse than losing was the humiliation I felt. I was a duck out of water. The average age in the fraternity was twenty-three. My son was the same age as many of these young people. "What was I doing here?" I asked myself.

I knew what I was doing here. Fulfilling a lifelong dream! I had always been involved in organizations, and so joining Beta Alpha Psi seemed like a logical step. The fraternity would give me an opportunity to meet recruiters and visit the offices of the major accounting firms in Houston, as well as a chance to make some friends at U of H.

I worked hard my first semester as a pledge and made several friends. They encouraged me to run for vice president. I knew I was a long shot but figured the worst thing that could happen would be that I lose. Nothing ventured, nothing gained. I decided to take the risk, but I had not counted on being laughed at. My self-esteem was still fragile from all the years of abuse in my marriage. The laughter hurt me.

The day after the election was hard, but several of my friends rallied around me and were truly embarrassed by the behavior of our fellow members. My hurt turned to anger. I decided to work even harder and run for office again in the spring. And I did just that. I started almost immediately by writing a technical paper to represent the fraternity and the university in a national man-uscript contest. It was my first paper of this caliber. I was afraid I would not do a good enough job but took the risk anyway. I spent the next two and a half months on my paper, even to the point of seriously neglecting my classwork. After the paper was submitted, I continued to put all my time and energy into Beta Alpha Psi.

Then, in April, it was time for elections again. I decided to run for president. This time I did not write a speech. Instead, I just got up in front of the group and talked to them about my plans and hopes for the fraternity. I was more relaxed and came across better. This time there were not any snickers or laughter. My hard work and dedication had paid off. I had earned the respect of the same people who just six months earlier had laughed at me. I won by a landslide. My election was only the beginning.

At our awards banquet, I was named the Most Outstanding Member. I also studied hard the last few weeks of school and did well enough on my finals to save my grade point average. Then, a week after school was over, I received a letter informing me that my manuscript had placed second in the national contest. It was the icing on the cake. The day the letter arrived informing me of my second-place finish, my ex-husband was going through another crisis. He had a bad fight with his girlfriend and he tried suicide again. He survived and was okay the next day. It was as though God was saying to me, "THERE is where you were, and HERE is where you are now!" Yes, I like my new life. I have put a lot of effort and work into my recovery to get to this point. God has been my constant companion and strength. The risking I have done has been hard, but in the end taking the risk was worth it!

Grieving is sort of like an onion: As you remove one layer, there is more underneath that needs to be healed. It is important to give ourselves the time to work on ourselves, whether that means grief work or just personal growth. And, as my next story illustrates, life has a way of letting you know you are not finished grieving.

THE GIFT OF TIME

The weather was so beautiful! The first cold front of the season had just arrived, and the sky was blue. There was a slight breeze, cool temperature, and low humidity, Houston's weather at its best! So why was I here, I wondered, instead of out enjoying the beautiful weather? I had gone through BE over a year ago. I had spent a year as an RSVP facilitator. Now I serve on the staff of New Perspectives' newsletter and The Journey Program. I had attended Arise and Walk conferences and many other programs that had helped me grieve and grow. So why did I feel so drawn to do a Beginning Experience weekend one more time?

By being honest with myself, I realized that I needed to finish the job! I am not quite finished with my grieving. This was brought home to me at my son's wedding a month ago. My ex-husband brought a girlfriend to the wedding. Even though it had been over two years since we separated and divorced, I had never seen him with another woman. The wedding had been planned for over a year. I had bought the perfect suit, had shoes and purse dyed to match, and bought new jewelry that added just the right accent. I had completed the classes required for my bachelor's degree at the University of Houston the day before and wanted to look as on top of the world as I felt! I wanted to celebrate completing four years of college as well as my son's wedding. I had many expectations!

I now realize I also wanted to pretend the dream was still intact. I was pretending that we were still a family. During the service, I was able to pretend since my ex-husband and I sat on the front row with my parents. I kept wishing he would hold my hand like he used to do when we were married.

It was a beautiful wedding, but the reception was very hard. I kept smiling, visiting with friends, and trying to be the "perfect" mother of the groom, but everywhere I looked, SHE was there—a constant reminder that our family was broken, that the dream was shattered! My ex-husband refused to appear in a video with me wishing Bill and his new wife the best. I grew more and more angry. Watching my children laughing and talking with her was so painful. I felt like they were abandoning me, too. I felt left out. I would have liked to have stayed longer, but the crowd had dwindled to just a handful of people and it was getting impossible to avoid HER.

When I got in the car, I exploded. Unfortunately, Susan was the recipient of my anger. Even after we got home, I continued to rage. I am not normally a person who rages. The only other time I remember feeling such anger was the night Tom told me he was leaving. Looking back, I see that some of my reaction was caused by fatigue. I had just finished an incredibly hard summer at school, having taken four classes and an independent study. In addition, my expectations had been too high, and my fantasy of a perfect family was unrealistic. But more than that, my anger told me I still had work to do. My unexplained fear was also perplexing me. I discussed my feelings with several friends, and one suggested I go to BE again.

So here I am! Do I really need to be here? *I wondered. As the weekend progressed, I let the magic pen*[25] *write and write. The writing helped me release the anger.*

---

25 Magic penning is writing down very quickly everything in your head until you have nothing more to write. This journaling technique lets you release thoughts that keep circling in your mind so you can listen to God's still small voice. I use this technique to write love letters to God. I start the page with "Dear God" then write until I have nothing else to say. I sign the letter "Love, Kathy." Then I write "Dear Kathy" and listen. I write whatever comes. Sometimes I do not hear anything, but sometimes very profound thoughts arise, and I continue to write until the thoughts stop. Then I sign the letter "Love, God."

The weekend has also affirmed how far I have come since my first BE weekend where I was still dealing with the acute pain of my loss. This weekend I was able to cut the final ties from my first marriage and feel totally free. I feel like I have completed this chapter of my life, and that a new chapter has begun as a whole single person. This new chapter is building on its own momentum and is providing a new foundation and structure to my life in place of the old. I now have friends, experiences, and opportunities. The memories will always be there, like old photographs in my mind, to remind me with bitter sweetness of my marriage. But the pain is gone, at least for today. It may come back occasionally, though it will be less and less. Now, as I sit writing this, the breeze blowing through my hair and the birds singing, I smile. My new life is so good. My heart is filled with serenity and joy. The anger and pain are gone.

The weekend worked its magic once again. The pain I have experienced in the past has made me stronger, made me real, and made me into the person I am today. I have healed stronger in the broken places.

CHAPTER SEVEN

MOVING ON

*A*fter *surviving the pain of divorce* and learning how to be a whole single woman, it was time to think about moving on. Here is a story of how I felt at the two-year anniversary of my divorce.

TWO YEARS AND COUNTING

I finally made it to that magical two-year mark. Everyone told me I would feel different, better. I was told not to make any major life-changing decisions and especially not to become involved in a serious relationship during the first two years after my divorce. Of course, I did not believe these caring people.

After my divorce, I wanted another relationship. I was okay. Maybe some people need two years to get over their divorce, but I was different. Or so I thought. I got involved in a serious relationship two months after my divorce. I was sure we were in love and meant for each other. I wanted to get married and have him move into my home. It would solve all our problems. He could help me with my bills and I could help him with his five-year-old son. He was a single dad. Luckily, my special man had more sense than I did. He had been divorced two and a half years at the time and did not take me up on my offer.

Luckily, during an RSVP session I discovered that my relationship had nothing to do with love but rather was my way of proving I could be a good wife. I was feeding my low self-esteem. I had to prove my ex-husband was wrong to have left me. I could cook, clean, and iron. I was trying to do all the things that I thought made a good wife. I did them all for my special man. RSVP opened my eyes and changed our relationship. I am glad to say we are still good friends, but I am also very grateful he was wise enough not to marry me. Changing the relationship after a hasty marriage would have been much harder and more painful for both of us and our children. I now understand why second marriages happen so quickly and why many of them fail. I learned that it feels good to stuff a new person, often one just like the abuser I had just left, into the hole in my heart. I call it the "divorce crazies."

I did continue my desperate searching, my own divorce crazies, for a new man to fill the emptiness in my life for at least another year. The hole my ex-husband had left was large and hard to face some days. The loneliness at night was especially difficult. I jumped into a couple of other relationships, thought I was in love again, and got hurt. Getting hurt turned out to be a real blessing. I withdrew from dating and worked hard just being with myself. I knew I had to change myself before I could enter into a healthy relationship. I had to develop new patterns in my life, so I would be attracted to a healthy person, not an abusive person. I eventually spent over seven years in recovery, from the time I became aware of abuse and began seeing a therapist and going to Al-Anon until I remarried. I worked hard to change.

I can now say I enjoy my own company. I have been going to Christian rock concerts alone or occasionally with friends. These concerts are something I really enjoy and want to do. I attend quiet days with my prayer group and take long walks with my little dog. I have come to cherish the free time I have when my daughter is away on Girl Scout outings or seeing her father. This is my time to be alone with me. To keep my own schedule, do my own thing, and just enjoy who I have become. I often stay home during this time now. When I was first divorced, I always filled the time she was gone with people. I no longer need to do this. To me, this is the goal of grieving. I felt I needed to come to the point that I felt comfortable with my singleness, the point where I was comfortable with myself.

At a recent Journey Program, we were asked to complete this sentence: "My life is like a cafeteria, when I go in _____." I completed my sentence with, "I always fill my plate too full!" My friends know that I keep my life very busy, with school, work, self-help groups, my daughter, and about a dozen other worthwhile endeavors. I like this hectic whirlwind I live in. In the past, I had kept this frantic schedule to avoid the feelings of fear and the abuse. Then after the divorce, I hid from myself and avoided being alone, always busy, never feeling or living. I would volunteer or pitch in at every event I attended to ward off the feelings of loneliness and help me feel that I belonged.

Now I enjoy life, with all its excitement, hard work, beauty, frustration, and joy, and feel each minute. I can sit and enjoy an event without having to be busy. I let others take a turn at the work. I enjoy just being there. I have worked hard to become a human being rather than a human doing.

In order to get to this point, I had to discover who I am. I had to overcome my low self-esteem and realize that I deserved to be good to me. If I don't, who will? Today I can be alone all day in my house without loneliness. I have discovered that there is a difference between lonely and alone. I used to be lonely when the house was full of people. There was no connectedness, no communication, no sharing, no ME! Now that I know myself and like being with me, I enjoy my own company. I am my own best friend. My time alone is special, not lonely.

Occasionally a lonely feeling still creeps back in. This usually happens when I return home late at night from a special event. I want someone to be there to share the experience with when I get home. Someone to talk to, laugh with, and care that I got home safely. Recently, after a very special evening I returned home too late to call anyone. As those old feelings of loneliness and isolation started to overtake me, I sat down and wrote a card to a friend. I put all the feelings I was experiencing and wanted to express into words. The writing helped.

I have other choices about how to handle my loneliness. I have many friends I can call. We often talk long into the night. I can chat with God. I can turn on uplifting music. I can write *in my journal. Or I can just ride it out. I have learned that I will survive my feelings of loneliness and be okay the next day. I no longer have to hide from loneliness or bury it under food or busyness.*

Fortunately, God has been with me and helped me navigate through these crazy first two years. When I have been very lonely, I have often envisioned Jesus holding me as I sank down in my king-size waterbed to go to sleep at night. It has helped, but real hugs help too. That is where all the programs, support groups, and people from my self-help groups helped in my life. The unconditional love helped me be kinder to myself, and their hugs carried me through many days afterwards.

I have learned to "hug" myself by being good to myself in little ways. Looking back on some of my crazy behavior from the magical two-year mark, I see I did need these past two years to heal and will continue to heal for a while longer. I was married over twenty years. I owed myself the gift of time to grieve the loss of this significant part of my life. Someone told me I needed to grieve one fourth of the time Tom and I were together, so I needed to grieve for five years. I thank all those who have gone before me and cared enough to try to help me. I only partially listened then, but now I believe. Two years do make a difference.

Another blessing was that my house never sold. My dad provided the money as an early inheritance, and with coop-eration from Tom, I was able to keep my home. Because my home is large, I have gained the opportunity to open it to peo-ple who need a place to stay or a warm environment in which to share a holiday meal. My daughter's friends have found a friendly, loving atmosphere for growth while struggling with the difficulties of becoming teenagers. Opening my heart and sharing my home with others has become an important part of my life.

The biggest gain that came through all my losses has been in my relationship with God. My spiritual life has grown dramatically. I have had the opportunity to attend several spiritual programs and expand my fellowship with other Christians. Living each day in total trust has brought miracle after miracle into my life. The greatest miracle of all is the joy I feel each day as I awaken to the wonderful, new life God is creating for me. In my life, God has caused all things to "work for good for those who love God, who are called according to His purpose" as it says in Romans 8:28. Through these challenges, my God has helped me to learn the real meaning of detachment with love, serenity, and patience. I know more challenges are ahead in my life, along with more losses, more pain, and more opportunities to grow closer to God and deepen my faith. As it says in Psalms 18:3, "Lord, my rock, my fortress, my deliverer, My God, my rock of refuge, my shield, my saving horn, my stronghold!" I have a firm foundation of faith that will help me through the next struggles life brings my way.

And just as the Velveteen Rabbit[26] discovered, it is only by experiencing life with its pain and love that we become real.

---

26 Williams, Margery, *The Velveteen Rabbit: How Toys Become Real* (Philadelphia: Running Press, 1981, 2017).

I like being real too much to let my fears stop me from living! So, I pray the prayer by Thomas Merton[27] that we said at the opening of each Journey Program:

My Lord God, I have no idea where I am going.

I do not see the road ahead of me.

I cannot know for certain where it will end.

Nor do I really know myself, and the fact that I think I am follow-

ing your will

does not mean that I am actually doing so.

But I believe that the desire to please you does in fact please you.

And I hope I have that desire in all that I am doing.

I hope that I will never do anything apart from that desire.

And I know that if I do this you will lead me by the right road,

though I may know nothing about it.

Therefore, will I trust you always

though I may seem to be lost and in the shadow of death.

I will not fear, for you are ever with me,

and you will never leave me to face my perils alone.

I continued my recovery and moved into a new phase with Beginning Experience II (BE II).[28] The following is my story of my first BE II weekend and how I continued to develop a whole single life.

---

27 Thomas Merton, *Thoughts in Solitude* (New York, Farrar, Straus and Giroux, 1958, 1999), 79.

28 Beginning Experience (BE II) was a weekend program that helped divorced and widowed persons become whole single people. See Programs Attended resource page at the end of the book for more information.

THE BREAKING OF DAY

After returning home from a New Year's Eve party, I read the following by Minnie Louise Haskins in my Daily Guideposts *devotional book:[29] "And I said to the man who stood at the gate of the year: 'Give me a light that I may tread safely into the unknown.' And he replied, 'Go out into the darkness and put your hand into the hand of God . . .'" That has been the past few years of my life: darkness of divorce, uncertainty in my own abilities, and fear of the unknown future. As I read on, the story ended with these words, "So I went forth, and finding the Hand of God, trod gladly into the night. And He led me toward the hills and the breaking of day . . ."*

Here again was my story. I was not always moving forward gladly. Sometimes it felt more like God was drop-kicking me through the next door. Nevertheless, going forward despite the fear "toward the hills and the breaking of day" made me think of my Beginning Experience II weekend. It was an awakening, the start of a new day, and a new chapter in my life as a whole single person.

I almost did not go to BE II. I was very busy at the time, and my childcare arrangements had fallen through at the last moment. God continued to tell me it was important, so I was finally able to make childcare arrangements and went. I had no expectations and was open to the experience. That weekend gave me the realization that I had passed through the grief from my divorce and emerged on the other side as a whole single person. I closed the writing time on loneliness with the following: "From

---

29 Guidepost Associates, Inc., Publishers, 1990. The poem, originally entitled, God Knows, was published in 1908, as part of a collection titled The Desert.

loneliness to solitude. What a difference it makes in your life!"
I am glad I have learned the difference!

My BE II weekend also awakened me to the fact that my
dream of helping battered women could now become a reality.
This dream had always been in the future. With the help of a
caring person in my small group, I realized that I was ready to
move on. Now, with my grieving behind me, I was ready to give
to others. I pledged to my group that I would call one of the local
women's shelters and volunteer for the hotline. I was helped by
two different hotlines when I was preparing to run away from
my abusive husband. Now I wanted to give back. When I left
BE II, I was excited about the new direction I had been given,
but I never dreamed it would work out so perfectly. I did the
legwork and reached for my dreams; God did the rest. He was
waiting to lead me "toward the hills and the breaking of day."

Last Thanksgiving my daughter and son were with me, but
this year they will again be with my ex-husband. I have had so
many ideas of things to do with MY third Thanksgiving since
my divorce. I am free to be me, to do something I want to do.
I thought about attending the singles retreat at Holy Name
Retreat Center,[30] helping in a food kitchen, or having dinner
with friends. Instead, I have decided to fulfill a long overdue
promise to visit my best friend in Michigan. I will call my
family on Thanksgiving Day. They are always in my heart. I
have the choice to make my holidays what I want them to be:

---

30   Holy Name Passionist Retreat Center in Houston provides hospitality, healing,
compassion, and opportunities for spiritual growth for all people.

happy or sad, full of people or full of pity, joyful or stressful. It is all up to me. After all, as Abraham Lincoln said, "Most people are as happy as they make up their minds to be." And I for one have decided to have happy holidays!

The planned trip to Michigan came with several surprises. First, my ex-husband decided he did not want Susan to come over, so a close friend, who was supposed to be house-sitting with my dog, ended up staying with Susan too. They had a good time, which included pizza for Thanksgiving, a favorite food of most thirteen-year-olds. And for me, I had a great time in Michigan. I especially hit it off with my friend's brother, who I had never met, which was a pleasant surprise.

Shortly after Thanksgiving, unbeknownst to me, across town a man was watching a John Hagee[31] video on finding a mate. He had raised his children after his wife ran off with another man and now was ready to live for himself. This man was taking Pastor Hagee's advice and getting down on his knees and asking the Holy Spirit to find him a mate . . .

Just before Christmas, a singles dance was held at a nearby church. I decided to go, but when I got there I did not know very many people. A couple of guys from The Journey Program with there, so I sat with them. Both spent most of the evening dancing with other women, but they did dance with me a few times. At the last dance, one of them, George, kissed me unexpectedly. In my mind I said, *What is this? He is obviously interested in this other woman so why did he kiss me? And he*

---

31 Pastor John Hagee is an American pastor and televangelist.

is not my type at all. Strange! They were gentlemen and saw me to my car. Christmas came and went.

March 1992 found me in a quandary. What am I going to do? Susan has a Girl Scout outing this weekend, and I have two center-orchestra, very expensive tickets to *Paint Your Wagon* at the music hall with country singer Dave Clark. And everyone I called was busy! Then I hear God whisper, "George?" "Are you kidding?" I answered. George was a man at The Journey programs who I sometimes talked to and occasionally danced with, but he liked my friend and another woman. Besides, he was just not my type. And if I asked him, I thought, he will think I like him, especially after the kiss on the dance floor. I did not want to lead him on. I was too busy to be involved with anyone.

I called another friend. Again, no was the answer. Again, God whispered "George!" Are you kidding! He probably has never even been to a musical! He is not my type. Is there someone else? God for the third time said, "George." Okay, I will call this other friend, and if he is busy, I will call George. You guessed it. My other friend was busy, so I called George. He answered on the first ring. Just my luck. I said I have this extra expensive ticket to the Music Hall. I asked him if he would like to go. "This is not a date," I quickly added. "Let us just say it is a business meeting. I will pick you up." He said he had never been to the Music Hall. *See God, I told you!* George said he would be happy to go but asked if he could buy me dinner. I said, "Well I expected you would since I paid for the tickets." Yes, sometimes I can be a brat, as God well knows!

We had a wonderful time, and Dave Clark and his band came out after the show and played a long encore. Well, that was the end. One date and we knew we were soul mates. He was funny and healthy. Different than I expected. The Holy Spirit had answered the man's prayer for a mate. Yes, George was the man who sent the Holy Spirit to find him a mate. I had been argumentative when God whispered his name but obedient—well, after some coaxing by God. I would have missed the love of my life if I had not been obedient. Great lesson to learn!

PS: If you hear George tell the story about the kiss on the dance floor, he says that he tripped, our lips just happened to meet, and he was lucky he did not break a tooth! Always the comedian.

At the end of August 1991, with my father's help, plus money from unexpected sources such as grants, scholarships, and part-time jobs that filled in the gaps each time my checkbook hit empty, I finished my coursework for my bachelor's degree in accounting. I had learned that many of the things I thought I needed were just extra baggage, weighing me down.

I was able to complete my degree in a total of four years instead of eight. As a summer graduate, I had to wait until May, 1992 for my graduation ceremony. Since I did not have a job, I stayed in school for the fall semester, taking two classes, which gave me time to study for the CPA exam. My study partner would arrive each morning, and he would keep me working all day, barely stopping for lunch. I was also going to a CPA exam review classes at night. My hard work paid off. In

November, I passed all four parts of the CPA exam. At the end of the Fall semester, I wrote this closing letter to my school life.

GOODBYE SCHOOL LIFE

Dear school life. Wonderful college years! How I have loved you. Every minute of growing and stretching; of my self-esteem improving; of intellectual stimulation and interaction; of making friends, close and casual; of setting my own schedule; and having the freedom to do many things! Yes, sometimes there was not any money and the bills piled up. Thank God for plastic!

Being president of the accounting honors fraternity has been great. I have seen my professionalism develop. I have gained a good understanding of the accounting profession and a better understanding of the world. The awards and recognition I have won have been wonderful, but sometimes my age still comes back to haunt me; to remind me that I have this all backwards; that I have a different view of the world than the majority of my fellow students. That the world has broken me, and I have healed stronger in the broken places. That I know what it is like to be real.

The offer of a fellowship from the University of Houston to get my doctorate is very tempting. How I would love to stay in academia with all my friends. I will miss them. I am leaving behind so many good friends. It is so tempting to stay, but after much prayer, I felt God had another plan.

I am not sure where this new door is leading, but I know I must go through it and close the door to my school life. A time that was rejuvenating. A time that was preparing me for my mission. At time for me to heal and grow stronger. A time of refining who I am through pain and tears, a time of stretching and building trust in my abilities. A time when I developed courage to face new challenges. I will miss the camaraderie I have shared with my fellow students. We have argued, laughed, and cried together. We have competed for grades and jobs. We have consoled each other and celebrated successes. We have accepted each other and shared the sense of pride that U of H is the best! Our school!

It is so sad to say goodbye. It is scary to be changing and not sure where you are going. However, there is satisfaction in having finally achieved my twenty-year goal of a college degree. Maybe it is a little late, but I did it, with help from my dad and my heavenly Father. Goodbye U of H and thanks. Love, Kathy

This letter proved to be premature. Just as the ocean ebbs and flows, so do the many openings and closings in my life seem to interact. For a few months, I had seen many new doors open and other doors close just as suddenly. I got an exciting job in the tax department with the largest and most sought-after of the Big Six accounting firms in Houston, but it did not start until September, which gave me time to do many other things. I never dreamed I would get a job with a Big Six accounting firm at my age. I was over forty! Ancient in their culture. I interviewed with all six of them twice and had a pile of rejection letters. This offer was truly a miracle.

With my new job starting in September, I could stay in school. I was working on my master's degree in tax accounting. I found the master's program very stimulating and challenging.

Staying in school and being the past president of the accounting honors fraternity opened other doors for me to serve on a regional and national level.

Another door that opened with the delay in the start of my new job was the chance to work as a volunteer on a hotline that helps women, especially battered women. I had pledged to call on my last BE II weekend and volunteer. When I first called there was a training session the next week, but the administrator was unwilling to let me attend because I was looking for a job and could not commit to a particular shift on the hotline. She finally agreed to meet with me and halfway through the interview, she said, "I am having ambivalent feelings about you. I am going to let you go through training without the required commitment to a shift." However, the miracle did not stop there. A week later, I got the job with the tax department of the large local accounting firm with the delayed start date of September, so I was free to make a nine-month commitment to the hotline. Wow! Was God working in my life!

Working on the hotline sometimes brought up feelings and memories I would have just as soon forgotten, but I knew I had to deal with them. This was another opportunity to heal. On my very first day on the hotline, I had to help a woman who had been beaten all night. She was in bad shape. I was trying to get her to leave and go to the shelter. I stayed on the phone with her for over an hour while she packed her things and got her baby ready. She said to me, "You do not know how much terror I am feeling." I could honestly say, "Yes, I do. I've been there." By the time we got her to safety, I was very pale and had to take a break. I was reliving my own feelings of terror and helplessness. But I had learned that there is help, choices, and open doors to go through.

Unfortunately, this door closed as fast as it had opened. I was dismissed from the hotline because my pro-life opinions were not in keeping with their pro-choice philosophy. This decision was made on hearsay from another volunteer and without any discussion with me. My supervisor was verbally abusive when she dismissed me. After many tears and much anger, I accepted this closed door, but still do not understand it. I found it very ironic that I had tried to help battered women only to find myself being battered again.

Thanks to my years of recovery, I was able to bounce back and move forward. I excitedly awaited the new openings and closings and trusting in God to continue to guide my steps each day. This next story is a summary of how I let go of my self-will and enjoyed my life as it flowered after my graduation from college.

MY RESURRECTION: A SECOND CHANCE AT LIFE

Before resurrection, there must be death. For me, this meant the death of my self-will. Self-will had always been a very strong character defect of mine. Even before marrying Tom, I felt I could fix him. I could make our lives perfect. If only I loved him enough, he would become the person I wanted him to be.

After many years of frustration and abuse, I became a robot, doing all the right things and portraying to the outside world a perfect family. Occasionally, the rotten inside would be revealed, but I would intensify my efforts to keep the perfect family image. In the process of focusing all my energy on what others thought, I lost myself, my dreams, my potential. Even my faith, which had been very strong as a teenager, shriveled up. My faith was still there as a tiny seed buried deep inside my shell. Finally, things got so bad that my life and my children's lives were threatened. All I could do was cry out to God for help. I was at the bottom. I did not know what to do anymore. I gave up my pride and self-will. My tiny seed of faith helped me to turn my life and my family completely over to God. Through the death of my self-will, I was given back my life, but not my marriage. What an incredible and sometimes painful journey God has led me on. I feel truly resurrected.

At the Arise and Walk Conference dance in February, after I told someone all I do, he asked me if I was trying to make up for the last twenty years of not living. Yes, I guess I am, I told him. I had obtained my dream of a college degree, a dream I thought had died. I passed the CPA exam. I have a wonderful new career starting in September. I have won awards, held offices in college, and had many new experiences I thought I was too old to have. I have accomplished other things that I thought I had lost the chance of doing.

Recovery has not been an easy road. The last few years have been filled with a lot of hard work. I have worked hard to get through the pain with the help of friends, family, grieving groups, therapy, books, and other programs that helped me *along the way. God has given me challenges I did not think I could handle, but with His help, I have.*

God continues to give me challenges. My latest challenge was a panel discussion on age discrimination at the regional meeting of my college fraternity. I was the moderator. But the scary part was my panel members. All four were national figures, very successful businessmen who specialize in recruiting and accounting. These men are powerful, knowledgeable, and articulate. I had tried to forget the idea of openly discussing the topic of age discrimination in a panel discussion. I had been blatantly discriminated against in the job-recruiting process because I was not in my twenties. But I did not look my age, so the firms assumed I was under forty and hence not protected from age discrimination. The Age Discrimination in Employment Act (ADEA) forbids age discrimination against people who are age forty or older.[32] The questions the Big Six recruiters asked me were, "Will you be able to keep up with the younger employees?" "How will you feel about a younger person being your senior and directing your work?" "Have you looked for a job in the oil industry? You would fit in better in industry where they would appreciate your maturity and past experiences." Basically, at that time the major accounting firms preferred employees straight out of college that were attractive, intelligent, and young so they could mentor them into the company's culture and make them successful partners over time. I did interview

---

32   U.S. Equal Employment Opportunity Commission website: https://www.eeoc.gov/laws/types/age.cfm.

with several oil companies and was offered two jobs, but these jobs did not offer me the same work challenges public accounting offered.

Once I got my job, I wanted to drop the issue. My new company would not be pleased with me exploring such a sensitive topic, but the idea kept coming back. The doors for the panel discussion opened too easily. I knew it was something I had to do, if not for me, then for the those graduating after me. However, I was scared and intimidated by my panel members!

The panel discussion went well. In fact, it was so well received that I moderated a similar panel discussion at the national fraternity meeting in Washington, D.C. This was another challenge I did not think I was up to but I was able to meet with God's help. Yes, my resurrection has meant a second chance to:

- ❀ Accomplish my goals

- ❀ Reach my potential

- ❀ Meet challenges and grow

- ❀ Love God more deeply

- ❀ Fulfill His plan for me

- ❀ But most of all, I got a second chance at life!

In May, 1992, I was named the University of Houston Outstanding Undergraduate the day before my official graduation. I led all my fellow graduates into the graduation ceremony. I was on top of the world. I felt like shouting, "I MADE IT!" I glowed with happiness and gratitude to God and my Dad for helping me accomplish a goal I had given up on over twenty years earlier. My mom was in the audience.

Sadly, my dad did not come. I was not surprised since he rarely came to mine or my brothers' events. Later he did apologize. He was disappointed. He said he would have come if he had known I was being honored, but I was told too late for him to change his plans.

That was the last time my mom came to visit me before her death. She wanted to stay with me and not go home to Dad. She was very ill, more than any of us knew, and exhausted. But after a few days she went home and made the best of the rest of her life. She died thirteen months later from a stroke after having a heart attack.

CHAPTER EIGHT

FLYING ON EAGLE'S WINGS

September 1992 was the three-year anniversary since that beautiful day when I became a free person. Fear has been a big part of my life and something I had to deal with in recovery. Sometimes fear still comes back.

Just before my second BE II weekend, I wrote this story of fear to share with the retreatants on the weekend. The story recaps some of my story that I have already shared and fears I felt in the past, both real and imaginary, that I have dealt with because of the abuse and divorce. The story also explores fears that I had as I moved forward.

OVERCOMING FEAR

The years I spent in my marriage were full of fear, sometime terror. There were times that Tom hit me in my sleep or raped me, so I had a deep fear of sleep. Many nights I laid awake. I ran away to escape the danger as Tom's abuse of prescription drugs and alcohol increased, making him more violent.

Living on my own with Susan had its own fears. I never had enough money to pay the bills even though I worked two jobs. We were living far from family and friends, without support. I feared I would not make it. I worried about Bill back in Houston with his dad. So after a lot of prayer, several months of recovery in Al-Anon and AA, I pushed my fears aside and trusted God that life would be better. My husband and I reconciled.

In hindsight, some would say that was a mistake, but when I look back on all that God did in my life and in the lives of my children, I know reconciliation was the better choice at the time. My son, Bill, who was in danger of not graduating from high school, graduated, and Susan was reunited with her friends. I was able to grow more during the time we were back together through a variety experiences, including going to night school. But then the abuse started happening again, followed by a layoff from my job, Tom moving out, and my life falling apart. So many fears! Where would I get a new job? How will I pay the bills? Would I lose my house? But God carried me through those and many more fears into a beautiful new life.

One of my therapists warned me that I would fall for a nice man after my abusive marriage. He was right. I am very attracted to nice men, and I did kiss a few frogs who did not turn into princes along the way. My fear of being abused again also manifests itself in my intolerance for drinking. I watch any man I date like a hawk. At the first sign of drinking, I get upset. Rationally, I know that many people can drink moderately and are not alcoholics, but I still feel the knot in my stomach when a man I am with has a drink. I begin wondering if I am overlooking "the alcoholic" hidden behind the "nice man" mask. I start questioning my judgment. I want to run away again. That is when I turn to prayer and faith to help reassure me. A favorite verse of mine is Psalms 34:5, which says, "I sought the Lord, and He answered me, and delivered me from all my fears."

Just before my second BE II weekend, I began experiencing a new fear. Paralyzing! Overpowering! All-consuming! At the time, I asked myself why I was so afraid. I know that faith overcomes fear. However, I was afraid down to my toes. Why? Of what? I did not know. I spent the weekend praying that BE II would again help. I was hoping that the writing and self-examination would enable me to touch the source of my fear. As the weekend progressed, I let the magic pen write and write, releasing my fears and doubts.

Tears! More writing! It became evident that the fears of making a wrong decision and not keeping my options open were again haunting me. At the next writing session, I explored my feelings about these fears and began to question myself. Am I afraid to totally commit to a new relationship? Am I afraid I am making a wrong decision? Am I afraid of more pain? I do not want any more pain! My writing continued.

I wrote, "Keeping my options open." Do I feel if I commit to this relationship, I will go back into "prison"? I felt I was in prison during my first marriage. A huge picture of the Statue of Liberty still hangs in my bedroom to remind me that I am free.

I love my life as a whole single person with the freedom to be me! The freedom to fall asleep at night without fear.

Other questions continue to fill the page. Am I afraid of losing the wonderful "Kathy" I have found so recently? Or is Prince Charming just around the corner, someone I will miss out on if I commit to this relationship? As the magic pen flowed, the fears started to subside and peace was returning. Naming my fears and doubts helped me overcome them.

Yes, I am afraid of closing the door on my single life. Afraid of leaving this part of my life I have so recently discovered. Afraid of saying goodbye to the ministries that have helped me heal and the growth, love, and friends I have found there. Afraid of possibly losing "me" again. Afraid of not keeping my options open. Afraid of making a commitment.

And the shadow of my old fear of abuse is still lingering there, too. My new man has an occasional beer. Is he an alcoholic but my denial is keeping me from seeing it? He told me he used to have a temper growing up. Does that mean he would someday abuse me? So much fear. I watch my new man's every action, always on the lookout for signs I might have missed.

But God brought us together and is in the center of our relationship. I must trust Him. Just having identified my fears has helped. Now I can face them and go forward. After all, I am not the same person I was years ago when I started recovery. I am not the same person who was so unable to cope that I ran out of work one day and went to an Al-Anon meeting in search of help. One of my old friends commented, "Some people say they have changed. Kathy, I've seen you change." I am keeping my eyes open. I am taking my time to get to know this wonderful man. I know God will be there regardless of what the future brings. Trust in myself and faith in God helped me through this fear. The weekend worked its magic once again. By Sunday morning, my serenity and joy had been restored. I had decided to feel the fear and go ahead with my relationship. There may be pain mixed with love in my future, but the pain I have experienced in the past has made me stronger, made me real, and brought me to the whole single person I am today.

As I grew closer to George, I learned many things. One is that men are sometimes abused too. George's first wife had a very strong personality. He felt abused at times. Another thing I learned was about intimacy, something I had not experienced in my first marriage because of the fear. I read a book and wrote a review for *New Perspectives* that answered the question, "What is intimacy?"

THE GIFT OF INTIMACY

According to Anne Wilson Schaef in her book Escape from Intimacy,

intimacy is:

❀ Knowing and being known by another

❀ Sharing information openly

❀ Not necessarily romantic or sexual

❀ Not confined to time and space

❀ Magical, beyond language, a hologram, a gift, and much more

This book helped me look at addiction and codependency as barriers that I had used to escape from intimacy. Schaef states that, "We have been taught in this society that in order to be 'intimate,' partners must be dependent. Dependency kills intimacy." In this book, Schaef defines and explains the underlying addictions of codependency: sex, romance, or relationship addiction. She believes these addictions are the root problems in failing relationships in today's society. Schaef contends that only after identifying and treating the underlying addictions can a person achieve true intimacy. She also states that "intimacy starts with the self, knowing the self, and being present to the self." Her prerequisites for intimacy, which she explains in detail, are:

❀ Loving someone by being a lover,

❀ while staying with yourself and

❀ fully participating in your own life.

Furthermore, in chapter four, Schaef gives a list of common skills many people have learned that lead to unhealthy, addictive relationships. A few of the items on the unhealthy list include:

❀ To be able to establish "instant intimacy"

❀ To have an instant physical or sexual attraction

❀ To know how to "compromise" personal needs, values, ethics, or morality for the relationship

In chapter six, she counters with a list of new skills needed for healthy relationships, which includes:

❀ To be able to "wait with" the evolution of a relationship

❀ To know that physical loving evolves as intimacy grows

❀ To recognize and accept one's own needs and honor them

She concludes by saying, "We have a whole new set of skills to learn if we are to have healthy relationships."

This book helped me in my journey toward being able to give the gift of intimacy and developing truly healthy relationships, especially with George. He treats me with respect and gives me space. He does not try to control me or isolate me. I am learning to grow into this healthy relationship. I am taking time to build a strong relationship with George, not rushing headlong down a cliff into a hasty second marriage. Attending a weekend for remarrying couples has been one part of achieving my goal of a successful second marriage.

In working toward my goals, I have also learned that my view of the road ahead is very limited. In the beginning, I had only wanted a college degree. God had a much richer plan for me, including a new career as a CPA. A loving and supportive group of single friends from the many programs I attended has been an additional blessing in recovery. I developed a deeper self-knowledge and acceptance and a stronger trust in God. Here is a story about my philosophy about goals and how God has led me through accomplishing some of my goals.

RIDING THE BICYCLE OF LIFE WITH GOD

Exercise more. Lose weight. Spend more time with my daughter. Pay off bills. Get the ironing done. Remarriage. A new house. Financial security in my old age. Success in my job. Cruising to Alaska. Law school. A storefront for battered women. Writing my autobiography. Goals or just daydreams? Yes, as this list above illustrates, I do have goals. However, for me, goals are not set or written down on paper. Rather, they are ever evolving and changing, an integral part of the way I approach life and follow God's guidance.

The following analogy explains my view of goal setting. I am riding down the road on a bicycle built for two. For the first part of my life, I was in front steering and doing most of the work. God was in the back, just along for the ride. I chose the direction we take and the goals for our trip; I did all the work. Things did not go well. Finally, I crashed and almost died because of my bad choices.

Not knowing what else to do, I let God take the front seat. He now guides my bicycle of life. This does not mean that I am just sitting in the back, watching as life goes by. No, I pedal, pedal, pedal. I do the legwork. I provide the energy, determination, and hard work necessary to reach His and my goals. I actively participate in my life. Sometimes, I do not like the path I must take to get to my goals. In fact, moving toward some of my goals feels more like God is throwing me right into the deep end of the pool instead of letting me tiptoe my way in from the shallow end. I often resist and put on the brakes. I sometimes like the rut I am in, even if I am miserable; my familiar rut is more comfortable than change. I find change frightening. The legwork required to change and reach my goals is hard and tiring, sometimes an uphill climb. But I have also discovered that through change comes a richer, happier, and fuller life. So, I continue to pedal.

After my layoff and my divorce a few years ago, I spent some time in confusion, depression, tears, and fear. In my grief, I lost sight of my goals. Desperately, I searched for a new job, but faced rejection after each interview. Then my friend helped me realize that I needed to trust that God knew where we were going. I just needed to keep pedaling, keep my eyes on the top of the hill, and let go of my pride.

Another goal I am currently pursuing is a position on a national board for an accounting organization. I have been pedaling toward this goal for two years now, and still have more work to do. This position is usually given to a very "typical" new college graduate, someone that is in their twenties and attractive. Because of my age, I am a long shot, but the path toward this goal has been exciting with opportunities to meet new people, expand my professional skills, and make a statement against age discrimination.

All my goals have been tied to the one goal that I actively chose for myself several years ago. I have pedaled very hard to get there, but without God guiding the way, I would never have made it! That goal is finding happiness, joy, and freedom, which come from within, from loving and accepting myself, from being a whole single person. With the completion of each goal, I often wonder what the view is like from the top of the next hill. And as I begin the next climb, letting God guide my path, I know that only the sky is the limit!

My recovery has changed. I am now in the stage of acceptance. I am building a strong life to move forward with a bright future. Here is a story of this new change.

COMING HOME THROUGH BEGINNING EXPERIENCE II

Another glorious weekend at Cameron Retreat Center. What a gift this place is to me. As the breeze gently sways the trees, I look up at the loving statute of Jesus in the inner courtyard. His hands are open and outstretched. He is calling me to Him, to heal, to grow, to serve. I am now serving as a facilitator on the BE II team.

What a different place I am in this weekend! In just six months, the collages I made at the beginning of each weekend

*have gone from reflecting a life that was like a powerful loco-
motive barreling by to one more like a quiet, cozy living room
filled with playful kittens. I was moving from a journey to a
home, from searching to contentment, from grief to joy.*

*I have discovered that joy is not feeling sad or happy, nor
is it getting what I want. Joy is my connection with God. A
contentment that gives me peace with myself even when life is
not perfect. When I began my journey of recovery years ago, I
claimed the positive affirmation, "Happy, Joyous, and Free." I
have felt happy and free for some time but have had only brief
moments of joy. Now joy is here! It is a wonderful sense of contentment with my life. Yes, there are still problems like never
enough money or time, and the stress of being a single mom.
But by learning to trust myself and totally lean on God, my fear
of the single life has given way to the wonderful joy of living.*

*For me, this weekend has again been a giant step in my
journey to wholeness. The discovery that I have gone from a
person who was searching and moving toward an unknown goal
to a person who is content, at peace, and at home with my life
and with ME has been such a surprise, the icing on the cake.
So, as a cricket sings his song in the grass nearby, I thank God
for pouring down His grace and mercy.*

I was so excited about my new job in the tax department at
a large local firm. Finally, someone saw my worth and looked
beyond my age.

The luster of my wonderful job at the large accounting
firm was short-lived. The week before I was to start, I got an

unexpected call from one of the lead partners. He wanted to tell me that the next day there would be a story in the news about the firm settling a lawsuit with the Equal Employment Opportunity Commission on age discrimination. He wanted me to know that the lawsuit had nothing to do with my hiring. I did not believe him. I was devastated to think I had only been hired to prove their case. As time went on, I realized that there were at least five other older students hired as well. But that was only the beginning. I was discriminated against and abused in many ways. The first was that I was not assigned any work—a death knell for promotions. When someone did give me work, I did my very best and eventually won over a few partners, managers, and seniors.

The younger seniors were intimated by me and would verbally abuse me as a way to show they were my "senior" in the company. I had to have my feet operated on and had to wear sandals instead of the required closed-toe shoes during my recovery period. One of the partners always made a point of staring at my toes in a disgusted manner whenever he saw me.

My age was hurting my chances of succeeding, but then I was called to jury duty. Not just any jury duty but a special federal grand jury convened to handle a particular case. I had to go the first week of every month. At the time, there was a long-term job located out of Houston that many of my peers were assigned to, but because of my jury duty, I could not be assigned to the job. So again, I sat without work. In hindsight, I see that God was in charge. As a single mom of a sixteen-year-old, it would have been tough to take an assignment away from home. God was watching over me, even if I did not see it at the time or appreciate it. I continued to try hard but spent a lot of time sitting around. In some ways, this was a blessing as I was finishing my master's degree at night and could study at work. As time went on, one senior saw my value and gave me work. I became a useful part of her team.

I will never forget when I finally got on one job and we had to work an all-nighter. I had been there over a year and never had to work an all-nighter. Wow. What surprised looks were on my peers' faces when they arrived the next morning and realized I had been there all night. I guess they thought someone over forty could not work all night! Not only could I work all night, I had many other talents and experiences that could have benefited the company if I had only been given a chance.

CHAPTER NINE

REMARRIAGE

Becoming a whole single person gave me the courage to marry again, but this time I let God guide me. I went through RCIA[33] to join the Catholic Church and completed the annulment[34] process, a requirement to marry in the Catholic Church. I found the annulment process to be another tool in recovery, helping me to see my part in the breakup of my marriage. After five years of single life, George, my wonderful Christian fiancé, and I were married in a beautiful Catholic Mass. Here is my story of my journey to remarriage.

---

33 The Rite of Christian Initiation of Adults (RCIA) is a process developed by the Catholic Church for prospective converts to Catholicism to gradually introduce them to aspects of Catholic beliefs and practices.

34 An annulment is a declaration by a Church tribunal (a Catholic church court) that a marriage thought to be valid according to Church law fell short of at least one of the essential elements required for a binding union within the church. An annulment has no effect on the legitimacy of children.

BEYOND DIVORCE

I have made it to a whole single life. I have even given myself the gift of fourteen months of not dating but just being my own best friend. I turn loneliness into aloneness. Now God is turning my world upside down again. Just as I got comfortable being single, God brought George into my life. What am I to do? Sixty percent of second marriages fail! I do not want to go through the pain of divorce again. I am afraid to risk marriage or even a serious relationship!

A friend tells me about New Life,[35] a ministry for remarrying couples. He and his wife had joined the New Life team. He shares with me that the team provided a support group for him and his wife through the rocky first years of remarriage.

George and I decided to attend a New Life event, just to see if we were right for each other. What a wonderful day. George and I are so much alike. The only major difference that surfaced was the way we put toilet paper on the holder! He does it over and I do it under, but for George, I can change!

A nagging doubt remains in my mind when the team couple talks about the "Romance" phase of a relationship, the period when everything is perfect. Is this the place George and I are in our relationship? Is that why the day went so well? Is that why I am sure I can change my toilet paper habit?

I remember the very first Arise and Walk Conference I attended. The keynote speaker talked about knowing someone two years before thinking about marriage. She said it takes that long to find out if they are a turkey. The story goes like this: The

---

35 New Life is a ministry for remarrying couples where one or both partners were married before. See Programs Attended resource page at the end of the book for more information.

first year they have on their peacock suit. They look good and handsome and decked out. Then the second year arrives, and the peacock starts to lose its feathers and you soon see the turkey. I named it the "two-year rule," and have handed out the story to friends I thought were jumping into new relationships too fast. Now it is my turn to take my own advice.

It has been over two and a half years now since George and I started dating. There is another New Life event next month. We are signed up to go. George keeps saying that we will have more to talk about this time. Does he have a hidden agenda? Resentments or concerns he has been afraid to voice?

The day came and went. Yes, George had an agenda. Several things he saw as problems in our relationship. After some honest communication, we both had a better understanding of the other person. Not all the conflicts disappeared; some differences will always be there. After all, we are two separate, unique people. New Life has provided us with many tools to resolve our differences, such as fair fighting. Fair fighting is a respectful, structured way of confronting each other on issues that are causing open or hidden conflict. It is a method for handling and resolving the differences of opinion that inevitably occur between spouses. Some of the fair fighting ground rules are:

❊ Remain calm. Try not to overreact to difficult situations.

❊ Express feelings in words, not actions.

❊ Be specific about what is bothering you.

�֎ Deal with only one issue at a time.

Physical harm is never considered fighting fair. Another truth New Life taught me was that you do not automatically love step-children like you do your own children. That helped me accept that it was okay not to love George's children immediately. To give us more resources, we joined the New Life team as facilitators.

Saturday will be our wedding day. We will wear small eagle pins on our wedding clothes to show that we are now flying like eagles. As it says in Isaiah 40:31: "They that hope in the LORD will renew their strength, they will soar on eagles' wings." The song "On Eagle's Wings"[36] will be sung during our wedding. I came to love that song that was sung often at the many Compassion Ministry programs. I had already chosen the song for our wedding when my mother died suddenly of a stroke. As the family met with the minister, my sister-in-law and I wanted "On Eagle's Wings" played at Mom's funeral, but my parents were Protestants, and Dad chose the beautiful hymns of their faith. During my mom's eulogy, the minister read the words of "On Eagle's Wings." As the mourners filed by the casket, the lovely family friend providing the music had her mother play the song. She picked up the words on the podium and began to sing. It was like my mom saying she would be at my wedding.

I was especially heartbroken that my mom died before my wedding. This message that she would be at my wedding was a beautiful promise from God. Later, there was a rainbow as

---

36 "On Eagle's Wings" is a devotional song composed by Michael Joncas. Its words are based on Psalm 91, Exodus 19, and Matthew 13.

we drove to the cemetery—another promise that Mom would be walking with my brothers and me during our lives. Henri Nouwen says in his book, Finding My Way Home *that:*

> Relationships are a mystery. It is possible to have intimate relationships with loved ones who have died. Death sometimes deepens the intimacy . . . I do believe though that after separation certain people continue to be very significant for us in our hearts and through our memories . . . I am a human being who was loved by God before I was born and whom God will love after I die. This brief lifetime is my opportunity to receive love, deepen love, grow in love, and give love. When I die love continues to be active, and from full communion with God I am present by love to those I leave behind.[37]

George's mother also passed away a few months later right before our wedding from pneumonia. She had Alzheimer's and was eighty-six. Watching Dad Wohnoutka cry at her funeral was another heartbreaking time. They had been married for over sixty-five years. "On Eagle's Wings" was sung at her Mass as well.

I am finishing this story when I should be doing many other things. This is my farewell to my single life. I am a little scared of the new chapter that is going to begin on Saturday, but I know it is God's will for my life. I love George. I feel strongly that God

---

37   Henri J. M. Nouwen, *Finding My Way Home: Pathways to Life and the Spirit* (New York: Crossroad Publishing Corporation, 2001), 137, 139–140.

has a mission for us as a couple. As the door closes on my single life, I remember what Romans 8:28 states: "And we know that God causes all things to work together for good to those who love God, to those who are called according to His purpose." My journey to becoming a whole single person has been hard and often filled with tears. Joy, freedom, and happiness have been my rewards. Another reward is being married to George, a wonderful Christian man, who prays with me and does not abuse me. Who lets me be ME! God has caused all things to work together for good in my life!

The following are two talks George and I gave as a team couple on New Life Retreats after our wedding. The talks sum up how far we have come and where we are now.

THE EVERYDAY ME

KATHY: *A few years ago, when my mother met George at my college graduation, she told him, "Kathy has been like this all her life." She was talking about the way I keep busy doing things and juggling many worthwhile projects at the same time. At times, overloading my life, but enjoying every minute. I continue to keep my life very busy with my career, family, volunteer work, and now with George and my two new stepchildren. I like this hectic whirlwind I live in. I enjoy life with all its excitement, hard work, beauty, frustration, and joy, and feel each minute. But I have learned to sit and enjoy an event without having to be busy. I have worked hard to become a human being rather than a human doing. George has helped slow me down, to take* *time to smell the roses, not just water, prune, and weed them. To take time to play. To let "Little Kathy" bake cookies or snap snapdragons or dance the night away in George's arms.*

GEORGE: *I was born on a cold winter night at a very early age in Bismarck, North Dakota. I came to Houston on a Friday night many years ago and got caught in rush hour traffic. I could not find my way out, so I have been here ever since. When people asked who I am, my answer is "A child of God." I did not always feel this way. I went to church, even when I was in Vietnam; but my heart often felt like a rock. Then one day, about fifteen years ago, God touched me. He changed my whole life. I became involved in many ministries and prayer groups. I went out every night to one meeting or another. Things have changed since I met Kathy. I am still a child of God, but now I just want to stay home with Kathy and our dogs, Scraps and Zeus. Job and home are about all the stimulation I can handle, what with two houses to maintain—hers, mine, AND ours.*

KATHY: *Twenty strings of Christmas lights adorn my home of sixteen years for the first time. My Georgie Porgie is the spirit of Christmas. From the small packages of cookies I found hidden in my suitcase when I arrived in New Orleans on a business trip to the six bars of Safeguard tied with pink fluorescent string all over the bathroom the day after I mentioned we needed soap, George is always giving. He is strong and quiet with a down-home sense of humor. George is my weatherman, fully equipped with the rain gauge and thermometer that now hang on the outside* *of our house. And my gardener, as the sweet potato vines taking over the entire backyard and the horseradish spicing up the flowerbeds, demonstrate. And George is my garbage man. He explained to me the importance of garbage on one of our New Life weekends. He did not feel I took garbage seriously enough. He is right! I have gladly turned that responsibility over to him.*

GEORGE: *I spent several years praying for the right mate. It got to the point that it did not matter anymore. I met Kathy at The Journey Programs. We danced together, and after a couple of years, we started going out. Actually, she asked me out first. I found that Kathy had some of the qualities that I did not have. She is well educated, enthusiastic, and likes to organize events. In other ways, we are very similar. She is a good Christian and very conservative. She also has good old country upbringing, having been raised on a farm in a large family just like I was. Kathy has solid values of honesty, integrity, dependability, and hard work.*

But she tends to push herself too hard and overdo. Kathy just finished her master's degree at night school while working full time, raising her daughter, helping others through the Catholic ministry to the widowed and divorced, and dating me. Now, she is learning to slow down and rest. To spend quiet evenings with me watching a good movie or visiting with our families.

KATHY: *George likes country music; I like rock and roll, especially contemporary Christian rock music. I had hoped George would learn to love my Christian rock music as much as I do. He has not, but he does accompany me to all my concerts. However, in* *other expectations I had, George has lived up or even surpassed my hopes. On our first New Life weekend, I learned not to expect stepparents and stepchildren to love each other automatically. Susan, my eighteen-year-old daughter, is the only one of our four children still at home. After our New Life training, I had expected George and Susan would have some disagreements after the wedding, when George moved in with us. What a surprise! They have gotten along beautifully and often gang up on me, with George taking Susan's side in mother-daughter debates on curfew or other teenage issues. George, having already raised two teenagers as a single parent, brings humor and a different perspective to these stressful times. We usually all end up laughing. George has also lived up to my neighbor's expectations. Before the wedding, George often came over and helped me with my yard work. One day my neighbor across the street asked me if George knew I was only marrying him for his yard work. I know all the neighbors appreciate my yard being mowed more than once every two months! And I enjoy not having to choose between a mowed lawn and a clean house.*

GEORGE: *My expectations include sharing the rest of my life with Mrs. Wohnoutka. I hope we can work in several ministries and grow old together. I want us to travel. At this time, we are only involved with New Life, but plan to branch out when, and if, we ever get settled. I had expected to move into Kathy's home in a couple of weekends and get on with our lives. Many truckloads of treasures, seven garage sales, and several months later, half of my possessions are still in boxes, and I cannot find the other* *half! But it is getting better. Kathy and I get to travel together three days a week when we carpool to work. This is a quiet time for us, away from the kids, dogs, telephone, and other distractions. Only the occasional lost soul driving down the freeway as though he owns it interrupts this special time. And we took an Alaska cruise in June, our dream belated honeymoon. A dream we both had before we ever met, and one expectation that we took steps to make come true.*

This next talk was about George and my faith journey and how God helped us find new love and a new life with Him at the center.

NEW LOVE, NEW LIFE

KATHY: *My mom was a Presbyterian and Dad was raised in the Church of Christ. Mom won out and we went to the Presbyterian Church as children. Sometimes Dad went with us, but most of the time he stayed home and worked on the farm. When I was ten we moved. Our little town only had a non-denominational church. I loved that little church. I also looked forward to going to church camp each summer. Church camp is where my faith in God grew by leaps and bounds. Then at the age of fourteen we moved again to a much bigger town. We returned to the Presbyterian Church. I was active in the youth group, helped with Bible School, and attended youth group. Several of my high school friends were girls with strong faith, some actually ministers' daughters, which probably partially explained why I always wanted to marry a missionary.*

GEORGE: *As a cradle Catholic, I was afraid of God as a child. I knew that if I did anything wrong, He would get me. The only difference between God and a priest was that the priest was close enough to reach out and cuff you. I believed that God saw everything I did wrong and kept score. My good deeds did not count. I always went to church. I knew I should. Even in the jungles of Vietnam, we had Mass whenever the priest showed up. He would lay under one Jeep saying Mass and we would lay under others. We would crawl one by one through the mud to take communion from him. I continued to attend church even after I moved to Houston. I felt I should. My faith in God was very small at this time. The first church I attended was like going to the cemetery on a foggy night. All very elderly people and here I was twenty-three and looking for friends. I tried a different church and continued to go there for the next twenty-six years.*

KATHY: *When I met Tom, my ex-husband, we attended an Episcopal Cathedral while dating. I thought Tom, too, had faith in God. It was important to me that we worship together, so I joined the Episcopal Church shortly after we married. Gradually, because of the abuse in my marriage, I shut down all my feelings, including my feelings for God. I went through the motions, but my faith dried up and seemed to disappear. For over fifteen years, I was a robot. It took Tom's suicide attempt and the children and I running away to save our lives, to bring me back to God. Through this crisis, I turned my whole life over to God, and the small mustard seed of faith hiding in my heart began to grow. Tom and I continued to work on our marriage with the help of counseling and twelve-step programs. Two years later, I was laid off from my job. Tom moved out, taking most of our money with him, and he insisted I put our house up for sale. Then the doctor told me I needed both my feet operated on. I was beginning to understand the Bible story of Job, and how he must have felt when home, family, livelihood, and health were all taken away! One night the reality of my situation totally overwhelmed me. I started crying and could not stop. I beat the bed and swore at God. I became more and more hysterical. After hours of crying, I was so exhausted—I just sat on the edge of my bed sobbing. I began to read a book of Bible verses for times of need. One verse gave me such comfort that I finally fell asleep. Romans 8:28 became my rock and anchor. Its promise, "And we know that God causes all things to work together for good to those who love God, to those who are called according to His purpose," has sustained me though many more trials.*

GEORGE: *At the time Paula, my ex-wife, and I married, my idea of God had not changed much. I always went to church and a couple of times a year the family would go with me. Then, God touched me in a powerful way. It was on Valentine's Day. I came home to find a heart-shaped roast on the stove with all the trimmings. I paged my wife and she called me back. When I asked her if she was coming home for supper, she said, "No, I guess not." All I could figure was she had gotten a better offer from someone. That crushed my heart and was the last straw. We had been having trouble for over a year. A week earlier, at a church meeting, a woman had said to me, "George, if you really want to find peace of mind, come to room 15 on Thursday night." So, I went. She was not there. I found myself in a room full of strangers. After singing a few songs and reading some Bible verses, they asked if anyone needed prayer. I said I did, and they prayed for me. God changed my heart. He filled me with peace. Now I knew God loved me and was not keeping score on everything I did. Each Thursday night I went and the group prayed for my needs. I knew God was going to change things in my life, and eventually He did. But not in the way I wanted, rather what was best for me in the long run. A year later, Paula and I were divorced, and I became a single parent, raising our two children to adulthood with God's help.*

Kathy: *After my divorce, I wrote a list of characteristics I want in my new husband and gave it to God. George fits that list. George and I were friends for two years. I never thought of him as a potential husband. Even after he surprised me with a kiss on the dance floor at a singles' Christmas dance, I was not interested. God knew better and kept nudging me until I asked George out. We have been a couple ever since. I had prayed for a man ahead of me spiritually. George is my spiritual leader. When I joined the Catholic Church, he was my sponsor. He gave me four dozen sweetheart roses for Valentine's Day, saying it was the only gift he could find worthy of me. George makes me feel like a virtuous woman as described in the Bible. God is the center and focus of our marriage. Our wedding consisted of praise music and uplifting readings to reinforce our commitment to God. He helps us solve our problems, shares our joys, and gives us hope. We worship and pray together and encourage each other in joint and separate spiritual activities. God is still my rock.*

GEORGE: *After eleven years of being alone, I had given up on finding a new wife. I heard John Hagee, a minister from San Antonio, talk on the Holy Spirit, the matchmaker. I quit looking and left the search up to God. Actually, I was quite content being a single person the rest of my life if that was God's will for me. Kathy and I always danced the last dance at The Journey Program. We were usually the only ones left to help clean up. I am good at taking out the garbage. She claims that I kissed her one night, but actually I just tripped on the dance floor and our lips happened to have met. I was afraid to ask Kathy out. She had a fancy little red car and a big house on the west side of town. I had a truck with over 250,000 miles of character and a tiny castle on the east side of town. Then she called and asked me to accompany her to the theater. Actually, it turned out to be a date. She tricked me, and we have been in love ever since. We try to put God in the center of our marriage, but sometimes we squeeze Him in a little too tight. Busy schedules, combining houses, and family crises have caused us to shortchange God.*

KATHY: *A priest once compared marriage to a rope. A rope that is made of two strands pulls apart, but when a third strand is woven in, the rope holds together as it says in Ecclesiastes 4:12b: "A three-ply cord is not easily broken." I see the covenant of marriage in the same way. George and I will hold together if we keep our third strand, GOD, woven into our lives. His covenant* *is fulfilled through our practicing the four graces of permanence, faithfulness, fruitfulness, and forgiveness in our marriage. George demonstrates his permanence to me when he dreams of the campground we will share as a retirement business someday.*

GEORGE: *As all marriages are to last forever, we both have said this is the last, until death do us part. I want someone to grow old with (I am almost there!), to spend my later years with, a wife that I can talk with, who has the same values and thoughts and desires that I have. Kathy is that person. Someone to be with through thick and thin. We want to travel and enjoy our grandchildren. Kathy shows her permanence to me by caring about my health and future. She works hard, plans for our retirement, and tries to get me to eat right and rest. Of course, I always have too much to do to rest!*

KATHY: *I am faithful to George in my appearance. On a recent Christian television program, Dr. Ed Young[38] said that one of the most important things to a man is an attractive wife. This statement made an impression on me and I try to always look my best for George, whether it is for a trip to the grocery store, a New Life weekend, or a wonderful night of dancing. Taking a few extra minutes to keep the date attitude toward hygiene and appearance is my gift of faithfulness to George. George has been faithful to my spiritual growth by encouraging me to become active in my prayer group again. He not only gives me the freedom to participate without him but also accompanies*

---

38   Dr. Ed Young is the senior pastor of the Second Baptist Church of Houston, Texas.

me to healing services and other programs the group sponsors for the whole church.

GEORGE: *As a Christian man, I try to be faithful to my wife, as I would be to God. The guys at work try to get me to go to a men's club with them after work, but I will not go. I have too much respect for Kathy to be going to places like that, and God would not be pleased either. But faithfulness is more. It is also being there for her in every need. Kathy attended New Life without me so I could go to the Promise Keepers Men's Seminar.[39] Her gift of time allowed me to grow and renew my promises of being a Godly man to her and our marriage.*

KATHY: *George demonstrates his fruitfulness to me by setting a good example of a Christian father for all our children and now our granddaughter. My children never had a close relationship with their real father, so George has been a Godsend to them. He has man-to-man talks with my son. His gentleness and understanding helps my daughter and my often-stormy relationship. As Susan puts it, "George keeps Mom calm." He also backs my decisions and consoles me when those all-too-often difficulties raising a teenager arise. George's fruitfulness has overflowed to my neighbor's, too. Since George moved into my home, the neighbor children love to stop in and talk with him and play with his dog Zeus. The other men in the neighborhood come by just talk while he is outside "tinkering." George genuinely displays the fruits of the spirit: love, peace, gentleness, and forgiveness.*

---

39   Promise Keepers focuses on helping men live with integrity through national conferences. For more information: https://promisekeepers.org.

GEORGE: *I feel that everything I do should benefit our marriage. Whether working in the New Life Program or some other ministry, we try to exemplify a good marriage. Kathy has faith in me and is always lifting me up at home and to others. She displays her fruitfulness in overseeing family events. She includes my children whenever possible, remembers birthdays and anniversaries, and reminds me to pray for them. Recently, during a crisis with Kathy's daughter Susan, we spent several evenings in prayer. I tried to support Kathy through this time without getting in the way. Supporting Kathy and our children is one way I pass on our couple love.*

KATHY: *The one spiritual gift I noticed about George first was his forgiveness. When we first started dating, I still had strong negative feelings toward my ex-husband. George would talk about his ex-wife as though she was his sister. In fact, that is how he feels. He has forgiven her for the hurts and unfaithfulness completely. George has had to use his gift of forgiveness in our relationship, especially in dealing with my outspoken family. After we had been dating awhile, I thought we should have a family dinner for him to meet my children and brother. As we were sitting around the dinner table my then sixteen-year-old daughter, Susan, announced that she was spoiled and that she was not going to like anyone her mother married. My son and brother added more injury to the situation by declaring that they would beat up anyone who touched Susan. I thought for a while our relationship was over. But George forgave their rudeness and decided I was worth the effort to learn to love my family.*

GEORGE: *Forgiveness comes natural for me. When Kathy and I seem to differ or get a little bent out of shape, I am always ready to forgive. I feel that saying, "I'm sorry" comes first. Then I am ready to ask Kathy to forgive me. I have learned that the words "I forgive you" have great healing power. Jesus even reinforced the importance of forgiveness when he said to forgive those who persecute you seventy-seven times. I believe this and try to act on it in my relationship with Kathy and others.*

KATHY: *In closing, we agree with the New Life Program. Our new marriage is:*

GEORGE: *A Risk*

KATHY: *An Adventure*

GEORGE: *A Journey*

KATHY: *A Friendship*

GEORGE: *A New Love*

KATHY: *A New Life*[40]

---

40 On Susan's 21st birthday, she told us she was pregnant. We told her we would help her raise the baby. In preparation for supporting her, we left the New Life team a few weeks later. Isaiah has been a joy. He often tells people he has three parents as he is more like a son than a grandson. He even called George "Papa Daddy" growing up.

And God continues to take surprising turns on the path of our lives, like the day in 1996 when He brought George and me to St. Justin Martyr Catholic Community. We came as visitors to a healing Mass, only to find a wonderful, warm community and an old priest friend of George's.

Other times, I still feel like God is dragging me along into new opportunities while I put on the brakes. Starting the Hannah Chapter of The Order Daughters of the King® at St. Justin Martyr Catholic Church was one such opportunity. God again surprised me. The name Hannah means grace, which reminds me of God's grace in saving my life. Through the chapter, He gave me a new daughter who needed an earthly mother. She is a beautiful young woman who was called to serve as my vice president. Her mother had been a Daughter of the King in the Episcopal Church, and she was following in her path by joining our Catholic DOK chapter. Months later, she told me who her mother was: none other than my friend who had been murdered many years ago. I burst into tears and we hugged. I told her, "I will always be here for you."

A few months later, I was asked to give a talk on the church's annual women's retreat in April 1998. I found it strange since I had healed and moved on from my abusive marriage. As I wrote my talk, I felt led by God to tell the story of my friend who had died, along with my own story. I also included how her daughter came into my life. I had never written about my friend before. I warned her daughter before the retreat that I was going to share part of her mother's story.

The retreat was full of God's power. On Saturday morning, I looked over at my friend's daughter and she was crying. Strange, but I was feeling her mom's presence. Did she feel it too? That evening, as I began my talk, there were over one hundred women sitting on the floor on blankets in their pajamas. The room got quieter and quieter as I read my story of abuse and recovery—except for my friend's daughter. She began to cry, not softly, but with sobs that got louder the longer I talked. Her sobs reached a climax when I told her mother's story and revealed our connection at the end of my talk. Everyone in the room realized I was talking about her mother.

As I finished and the strains of the closing song began to play, I looked up.

There, over the door across from me was my friend's spirit. She smiled at me and left. I then knew I was not there to tell my story, but to help her daughter heal. When I talked to her daughter later, she said that she had felt her mother's spirit was there all day. I confirmed her feelings by saying, "Yes, she was." Then she told me that the date of the retreat was the seven-year anniversary of her mother's death. Wow! God does work in mysterious ways! She also told me that the song I chose to close the talk was her mother's favorite, something I did not know. Her mother and I had both found strength to trust God during our struggles to get free from our abusers in this very special song, "Learning to Trust," by David Meece.

EPILOGUE

Life goes on. One of the tax partners who taught part time at U of H and was one of my professors was promoted to the controller position in the firm. He needed someone with tax experience to handle the taxes of the consulting side of the business. So, I took the job in payroll. I was basically demoted. But one thing I had access to was the payroll records, and in checking the salaries of those of us who were still there and had been hired in defense of the lawsuit, I found we were all paid significantly less than our peers. As part of the lawsuit, those of us who were hired had to talk to the Equal Employment Opportunity Commission (EEOC) twenty-four months afterwards. The partners implied we needed to be "company" people. I did not say much—just answered the EEOC's questions truthfully.

While working in payroll, one of my coworkers, a very young woman, was rude and demanding to one of the consulting employees. The young man who was the recipient of the hostility had not turned in his time sheet because he was away at his dying mother's bedside. My coworker kept calling him and was very rude when he finally brought in the time sheet after his mother lost her battle with cancer. I tried to talk to her, but she did not understand his feelings. I prayed for her to develop some empathy for the young man and others who suffered loss. I, too, had lost my mom when she was too young, just sixty-four. Two weeks later my coworker's father died suddenly of a heart attack. He was forty-eight. All of us treated her with kindness and empathy. She changed and developed empathy and kindness toward others. My own experiences of abuse, divorce, and loss have made me stronger and given me empathy for others who are suffering. The world did break me, just like it does most of us, but I healed stronger in the broken places so I could help others.

Gradually, I got acquainted with the consulting employees and they liked me. They saw my age and life experiences as an asset. When they won a large contract to set up an accounting center for a large international company in Houston, I was able to cross over the "Chinese Wall," as we called the division between the two firms. It was nearly impossible to cross over. If it had been easy, many would have crossed over. The consulting side of the company had a relaxed dress code and work that was varied and challenging. Again, God's hand was there, as I became the general ledger administrator on the Oracle accounting system, partly because I had previous experience in accounts payable and receivables.

Then, after a year and a half, another door opened. The international company was going to upgrade their Oracle accounting system. I asked to go to training. My manager agreed to pay for the training, but I had to pay my own expenses. The training was in Dallas, so I drove up and stayed with George's son and his family.

The first day of class, I got lost and arrived late. There was only one seat left in the very back row. I am a front-row person! There was an annoying extra Oracle person in the class who would roll his chair up and join my partner and me during lab times. He talked a lot which was distracting. Over the week, we had lunch and I found out he was a new manager at Oracle. He offered me a job! I said no, because it would involve traveling 100 percent of the time, leaving little time at home with George.

After I returned home, he continued to call me and try to talk me into taking the job. Then, my boss called me and told me the promotion I had been promised was not going to happen. My boss said everything was running so well they were eliminating the position. Everything was going smoothly because I had been doing all the work of my previous boss plus mine for several months. I was very upset. When I got home, George said I should call back the man from Oracle.

So, I did. It took two months of interviews and a trip to Denver before the job offer came through. God's hand was guiding me all the way, and when they offered me a 65-percent raise, I knew I was to take the job. Here is the letter I gave my manager.

NOVEMBER 10, 1997

It is with a sad heart that I hereby resign as an accountant effective Friday, December 5th, 1997. I will miss the many friends I have made over the past year and half. I will also miss being affiliated with this firm, as they were the only one to give me a chance when I graduated from college late in life. I appreciate the start they gave me and will always think favorably of the organization.

I have approximately four days of vacation left. I would like to take off Fridays, November 14th and 21st and Wednesday, November 17th to tend to personal business.

On December 8th, I will be joining Oracle Education as an instructor. I did not actively seek this job, but when the opportunity was presented to me, it was too good to turn down, both financially and career wise. Oracle has been very understanding of my personal need to give four weeks' notice rather than the normal two weeks. The extra time will help me transition my current workload.

SINCERELY,

KATHRYN M. WOHNOUTKA

I wish I had a picture of my boss' face. I had not even hinted to anyone I was interviewing. He started to say something, and I interrupted him. I said, "You should have given me the promotion I was promised and the raise. Now it is too late."

I had closed the general ledger books for 1996 on February 23, 1997, well before the end of the first quarter. When I talked to one of my old coworkers a few months later, they still had not closed the books for 1997 on April 13, 1998, two weeks past the end of the first quarter. The parent company was very meticulous about making quarterly reporting deadlines with the SEC and other stakeholders, so I am sure there were some unhappy folks at missing the first-quarter reporting deadline. It also took three people to replace me. It would have been cheaper for them to give me my raise. Oh well, God is in charge of my life and He had better things in mind for me. In addition, the annoying man from class was my manager for four years. He was a great manager and I learned a lot from him. Unfortunately, he died too young from cancer a few years later.

And on December 8, 1997, as I walked into my first Oracle class as an employee, I closed the door on my previous life. God and I are now on to new joys, sorrows, healing, and growth. Stay tuned for book two, *But God, I Am an Accountant,* which contains the stories of my new life after remarriage, sprinkled with humor and mysticism, growth and miracles, sorrow and Franciscan joy, and adventures on God's path to wholeness.

Dear readers, one last note. I started the book with a pro-life story. Why am I pro-life, you may ask? I am pro-life because I have had the joy of carrying two children in my womb—of feeling them kick and move and be a part of me while at the same time being separate little people. I have had the joy of watching them grow into talented, caring people, both serving others in their own ways. Susan with empathy and caring for the underprivileged high school students with food, a listening ear, and skills to help them go to college; Bill saving lives as an EMT, paramedic, and now an emergency room nurse.

I have also had the joy of watching my grandchildren grow and mature: Bill's three children, Courtney, Tad, and Erin, and Susan's son, Isaiah. All of them have had their challenges and at times life has been tough. Their parents have made many sacrifices for them. Bill's wife Sara brought two handsome boys into our lives, Tyler and Colby. Tyler and his wife Melissa have blessed us with our first great-grandson. George came with two wonderful children, Steve and Crystal, and their spouses, Sheila and David, and six more grandchildren. In total, nine boys and three girls.

Now that my grandchildren are reaching adulthood, their potential is shining through. Courtney is a kindergarten teacher and has a special gift for helping children who are struggling with behavioral problems. Courtney and husband Jason blessed us recently with our second great-grandson. Tad, who has worked as a pharmacy technician since high school, is still in college and plans to be a doctor. Erin, with her beautiful smile and cheerful attitude, followed her father Bill and sister Courtney's example and went to Costa Rica to serve the poor with Amigos while in high school. Now, after graduating from high school, she has gone into the Marines to defend our country. I always thought it would be one of the grandsons, not my youngest granddaughter, who joined the military.

Isaiah creates beautiful art and teaches little ones to swim. For his sixteenth birthday, he wanted to help a homeless man he saw often on the street. He told me, "Grandma, you can tell he is homeless. He always has on the same clothes." He filled one of his backpacks with food, some of his clothes, water, first-aid items, and some of his money to give to the man. His kind heart also recently helped a young, single mother who did not make enough money to buy Christmas gifts for her four-year-old daughter. Isaiah had the mother put what her daughter wanted on Amazon. Even though he was only working part time, he bought all the gifts for her to give to her daughter.

In summary, for me, being pro-life is not political, a cause, or obedience to my church's teachings. It is about my personal experiences of love and joy from the children, grandchildren, and other people I have been blessed to know. It is about the lives I have seen changed, the good that has been done in the world by each one of them, and the belief that every fertilized egg is a beautiful beloved child of God with a special place in the world. Each one has a special job to accomplish that no one else can do, a special way of changing the world for the better.

Blessings . . .
Kathy

PROGRAMS ATTENDED

The Compassion Ministry of the Archdiocese of Galveston-Houston sponsored many programs. Sadly, most of these programs have faded out over the last twenty-five years, but there are other similar programs and events for those who are grieving. The internet is a good tool to find the current programs, or you can reach out to your church. Each person is different and what worked for me may not be the answer for you, but I hope I am giving you the courage to reach out. The programs I wrote about included:

❀ The Journey Program: A quarterly program to help divorced and widowed. The program began at 1:00 pm and ended at midnight. It included Mass, two speakers, a priest and a therapist skilled in grief counseling, small group sharing, and a dance in the evening after dinner on your own.

❀ Response Support for Valuable People (RSVP): A support program for the recently separated, divorced, or widowed which met for ten successive weeks in the evening. The program included talks shared by the team members who had all been through loss of a spouse, writing on the topic for the evening, and small group sessions.

❀ Arise and Walk Conference: An annual conference for the widowed and divorced that lasted for two days and featured speakers on grieving, interactive workshops, and a dance the last evening.

❀ *New Perspectives*: A monthly newsletter for the divorced, separated, and widowed that advertised singles ministry events. The newsletter contained stories by those suffering from loss and participating in recovery.

❀ Beginning Experience (BE): A weekend retreat to help bring closure to a relationship and is offered in many places around the country. The team shares their stories of loss, and there is writing in response to questions related to the talk theme in addition to small group sharing. BE was under the umbrella of the Compassion Ministry but was actually a separate, worldwide program that still exists in some places today. See their website: https://beginningexperience.org/program/beginning-experience-weekend/.

❀ Beginning Experience II (BE II): A weekend program created by the Compassion Ministry to help divorced and widowed people become whole single people by concentrating on issues of being single such as loneliness, sex, and friendships. The weekend format was very similar to Beginning Experience, with talks by the team, writing, and small group sharing.

❀ New Life: A one-day program for remarrying couples where one or both partners were married before. Included talks by the team, writing, sharing between the partners, and small group sharing with other couples. New Life is similar to Engage Encounter (see their website at: https://engagedencounter.com).

WORKS CITED

Colgrove, Melba, Harold H. Bloomfield, and Peter McWilliams. *How to Survive the Loss of a Love.* New York: Bantam Books, 1976, 2006.

Fisher, Bruce. *Rebuilding: When Your Relationship Ends.* San Luis Obispo: Impact Publishers, 1989, 2016.

Gill, A.L. *God's Promises for Your Every Need.* Houston: J. Countryman, Publishers, 1981, 2008.

Kline, Donald L. *Susanna Wesley: God's Catalyst for Revival.* Lima, OH: C.S.S. Publishing, 1980, p. 42. Taken from Richard Foster. *Streams of Living Water.* San Francisco, Harper, 1989, p. 237.

Kübler-Ross, Elisabeth and David Kessler. *On Grief & Grieving: Finding the Meaning of Grief through the Five Stages of Loss.* New York: Scribner, 2005, 2014.

Merton, Thomas. *Thoughts in Solitude.* New York: Farrar, Straus and Giroux, 1958, 1999.

Neeld, Elizabeth Harper. *Seven Choices: Finding Daylight after Loss Shatters Your World.* New York: Grand Central Publishing, 1990, 2003.

Newell J. Phillip. *Christ of the Celts: The Healing of Creation.* San Francisco: Josey-Bass, 2008.

Nouwen, Henri J. M. *Finding My Way Home: Pathways to Life and the Spirit.* New York: The Crossroad Publishing Company, 2001.

Schaef, Anne Wilson. *Escape from Intimacy: Untangling the Love Addictions: Sex, Romance, Relationships.* New York: Harper Collins Publishers, 1990.

Wiesel, Elie. *Souls on Fire: Portraits and Legends of Hasidic Masters.* New York, Simon & Schuster Paperbacks, 1972, 1982.

Williams, Margery. *The Velveteen Rabbit: How Toys Become Real.* Philadelphia: Running Press, 1981, 2017.

ABOUT THE AUTHOR

*K*athryn *Wohnoutka, OFS,* is a member of the Secular Franciscan Order, the third branch of the Franciscan Family, and a spiritual director. She often presents workshops and days of reflections on spiritual gifts, simplifying your life, forgiveness, Franciscan evangelism, and other topics for groups in various parts of the country. She has served as the spiritual director and speaker at numerous women's retreats guiding women to healing.

Kathryn is a CPA and has served on boards and finance committees of several nonprofit organizations. She works full time for Oracle Corporation, where she manages a group of curriculum developers. She and her husband, George, live in Katy, Texas. They are blessed to have four grown children, twelve grandchildren, and two great-grandsons.

As Kathryn closes the door on her previous life, she is embarking on a new journey with joys, sorrows, healing, and growth. Stay tuned for her second book, *But God, I'm an Accountant,* which contains the stories of her life after remarriage, sprinkled with humor, mysticism, miracles, Franciscan joy, and adventures on God's path to greater wholeness.

Made in the USA
Columbia, SC
18 December 2021

52013283R00112